THE COMPLETE GREAT WORLD CHALLENGE

Vinita Zutshi's fascination with words led to her becoming a writer. She enjoys writing both fiction and non-fiction for children and adults, and has created innovative formats in personalised writing. *The Complete Great World Challenge* was born from her daughter's enchantment with the social sciences—and Vinita's ignorance of it!

Find out more about her work on *www.vinitazutshi.com.* You can contact her at *vinita@vinitazutshi.com.*

Published by Scholastic India Pvt. Ltd.
A subsidiary of Scholastic Inc., New York, 10012 (USA).
Publishers since 1920, with international operations in Canada, Australia, New Zealand, the United Kingdom, India, and Hong Kong.

For information regarding permission, write to:
Scholastic India Pvt. Ltd.
A-27, Ground Floor, Sigma Centre
Infocity-1, Sector 34, Gurgaon 122001 (India)

This edition: May 2017

Reprint : 2018, 2019, 2020

ISBN-13: 978-93-5275-070-2

Printed at Shivam Offset Press, New Delhi

The Complete Great World Challenge

Vinita Zutshi

Illustrated by
Soumesh Choudhury

SCHOLASTIC
New York Toronto London Auckland
Sydney New Delhi Hong Kong

For ______, because.

Acknowledgements

Thanks are due to many who helped in the course of writing this book:

Dr Neha Narula, Dr Garima Trehan and Dr Parul Hellan of Qi Spine for putting my back on its feet.

Minakshi Khemka for friendship, food, laughter and so much more.

Jai, Mona and my parents—you keep it sane and you make it crazy, in near-perfect proportions.

Contents

1. HIDDEN CAPITALS

Find the Asian capitals hidden in these sentences.

1. Chairman Amarillo declared the meeting closed.
2. Erica, Stan and Fred were good friends.
3. Tom, us cats must learn to stay together.
4. Have you noticed how Anushka bullies her little brother?
5. Martha, no, I don't think geishas are from Russia.
6. Do you know what happened in Jallianwala Bagh, Dad?
7. Madam, as customs change, we are forced to change along with them.
8. My friends' names are Vincent, Ash, Ken, Trent and Adam.
9. Oedema leaves us bloated and lethargic.
10. What a score it was—Panama nil and Uruguay three!
11. Do habits make us or do we make our habits?
12. Enrico, Lombok is an island in Indonesia.

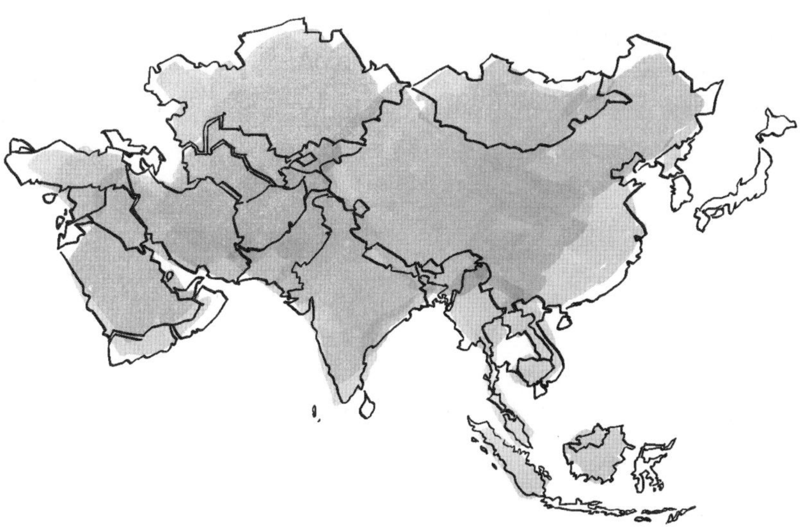

ASIA

2. MONEY JOINS HANDS

Join two letter groups from the box below to make the currency names of the following Asian countries.

SO	KY	HAM	GE
PO	HT	AT	ONI
TEN	RIK	DO	K
DR	IP	AM	ON
TUG	SOM	W	BA
DIR	UND	NG	M

1. Syria – _______________
2. Kyrgyzstan – _______________
3. Laos – _______________
4. North Korea – _______________
5. Myanmar – _______________
6. Armenia – _______________
7. Kazakhstan – _______________
8. Mongolia – _______________
9. Thailand – _______________
10. Tajikistan – _______________
11. United Arab Emirates – _______________
12. Vietnam – _______________

3. FLORAL BOUQUET

Each set of letters here has the name of an Asian country and its national flower hidden away. Can you identify the country and its national flower? The first letter in each clue is also the first letter of the country's name.

1. I L N O D T I U A S
2. I R R O A S Q E
3. V R I E D E L T O N A T U M S
4. B B H L U U E P T O P A P N Y
5. A T F U G L H A N I I S T A P N
6. N M O A R G T N H O K L O R I E A A
7. N R H E O D P O D E N A D R O L N
8. I C S Y C R L A A M E E L N
9. J B O L A R C D K I A R I N S
10. S J Y A S R M I I N A E

ASIA

4. CHINESE RULE

Hidden in the grid are the names of 10 Chinese dynasties. Strike off the names vertically, horizontally and diagonally.

S	R	G	Q	I	N	K	T	T
O	H	N	Y	I	M	G	L	D
A	Q	A	X	I	Q	Q	P	Y
I	P	T	N	I	S	O	N	G
L	K	G	N	G	Z	H	O	U
N	B	G	P	N	A	U	Y	X

ASIA

5. BEASTS OF PRIDE

Unscramble the animal and bird names, in the second column, to find the national animals and birds of various Asian countries.

Country		Scrambled Up		National Animal/Bird	
1.	East Timor	a.	LOCERICOD	i.	East Timor – Crocodile
2.	South Korea	b.	ETGIR	ii.	______
3.	Japan	c.	SHANPETA	iii.	______
4	Lebanon	d.	OXENHIP	iv.	______
5.	Nepal	e.	OWC	v.	______
6.	Israel	f.	OOHOPE	vi.	______
7.	Qatar	g.	ROXY	vii.	______
8.	Laos	h.	TEPELHAN	viii.	______
9.	Palestine	i.	BRISDUN	ix.	______
10.	Cambodia	j.	ANGTI BISI	x.	______

6. WHOSE BOOK IS IT?

Match the names of the religious books, in the first column, with the religions they belong to, in the second column.

Book		**Religion**	
1.	*Guru Granth Sahib*	a.	Islam
2.	*Bhagvad Gita*	b.	Bahai Faith
3.	*Quran*	c.	Christianity
4.	*Bible*	d.	Sikhism
5.	*Talmud*	e.	Buddhism
6.	*Zend-Avesta*	f.	Hinduism
7.	*Kitab-i-Iqan*	g.	Zoroastrianism
8.	*Dhammapada*	h.	Judaism

7. MY PIECE OF COUNTRY

Each three-letter group, given below, is part of an Asian country's name. Can you identify these countries?

	3-letter group	**Country**
EXAMPLE:	**NDI**	**INDIA**
1.	ANM	____________
2.	APO	____________
3.	IWA	____________
4.	TNA	____________
5.	EME	____________
6.	ANO	____________
7.	ONG	____________
8.	UWA	____________
9.	AKI	____________
10.	RAI	____________
11.	ODI	____________
12.	LAD	____________
13.	ONE	____________
14.	PIN	____________
15.	MEN	____________

ASIA

8. INCLUSIVE INVENTIONS

The name of each Chinese invention contains a word that fits the clue in that line. To find this word, cross off the extra letters in the invention's name and read the remaining letters from left to right.

	Invention	Clue	Answer
	EXAMPLE:		
	~~S~~ A ~~L T~~ P E ~~T R E~~	**Common name for chimps, gorillas, etc.**	**APE**
1.	Coffin	Opposite of 'on'	________
2.	Porcelain	Water falling from the sky	________
3.	Pendulum	A type of tree	________
4.	Abacus	A mode of public transport	________
5.	Acupuncture	Clean, good or unmixed	________
6.	Pottery	A mammal who is comfortable in water	________
7.	Marshmallows	The limbs attached to your shoulders	________
8.	Gunpowder	Below	________
9.	Flamethrower	Not early	________
10.	Chopsticks	The one who has invited you home	________
11.	Forged steel	What you need to do when you're tired	________
12.	Gas cylinder	Opposite of 'loss'	________

9. FIVE-LETTER CITIES

Hidden in the grid are the names of Asian cities, made of five letters. Strike off the names vertically, horizontally and diagonally. A letter may be used more than once. Read the uncrossed letters in order from left to right to find the name of another Asian city.

M	A	C	A	U	A	Y	Q
P	A	C	C	E	M	D	U
D	E	L	H	I	M	N	K
L	L	T	E	O	A	A	A
U	U	Z	R	N	N	K	B
O	S	A	K	A	T	A	U
E	O	O	N	H	A	H	L
S	M	C	I	T	P	D	Y

Uncrossed letters: __ __ __ __ __

ASIA

10. LARGE DESERTS

Fill in the blanks to make words. Then, read down the blanks to get the names of two deserts in Asia.

_ AYAK (a type of boat)
_ FTER (once something is over)
_ OAD (on which to drive)
_ LTER (to change)
_ NEE (a joint in the leg)
_ PPER (not lower)
_ ILE (measure of distance)

_ RUNK (chest made of metal)
_ MBER (colour of traffic light)
_ NIFE (you cut with this)
_ LAMA (an animal resembling a camel)
_ NGRY (annoyed)
_ EAL (what you eat)
_ PPLE (one a day keeps the doctor away)
_ ING (man of royalty)
_ CHE (pain)
_ IBBLE (eat in tiny bites)

— — — — — — —
Desert (Turkmenistan)

— — — — — — — — — —
Desert (China)

11. BOOKED!

Each book listed here is set in a different Asian country. Match the book with its author and the country where its story is set.

	Book	Author	Country
1.	*And the Mountains Echoed*	Lian Hearn	Israel
2.	*The Good Earth*	Graham Greene	Vietnam
3.	*Exodus*	Han Suyin	Pakistan
4.	*Moth Smoke*	Amitav Ghosh	China
5.	*Across the Nightingale Floor*	Leon Uris	Myanmar
6.	*Swami and Friends*	Khaled Hosseini	Bangladesh
7.	*The Quiet American*	Tahmima Anam	Japan
8.	*The Mountain is Young*	Pearl S Buck	India
9.	*A Golden Age*	Mohsin Hamid	Nepal
10.	*The Glass Palace*	R K Narayan	Afghanistan

ASIA

12. PRIZED PEOPLE

Fill in the blanks to find the names of Asian Booker or Man Booker-winning authors. Reshuffle the letters in the filled blanks, in the space given below, to find the name of an Asian author who won the Nobel Prize for Literature in 2006. His books include *Istanbul, Snow, My Name is Red,* and *The Museum of Innocence*.

1. _ ICHAEL O _ NDATJE
2. A _ UND _ ATI ROY
3. S _ LMA _ RUSHDIE
4. _ AZUO ISHIG _ RO
5. RUTH _ RAWER JH _ BVALA

Winner of the Nobel Prize for Literature in 2006: _ _ _ _ _ _ _ _ _ _

13. ATOP THE MOUNTAIN

Arrange the names of Asian peaks listed below into the grid and read the shaded column top down to find out the name of an Asian volcano.

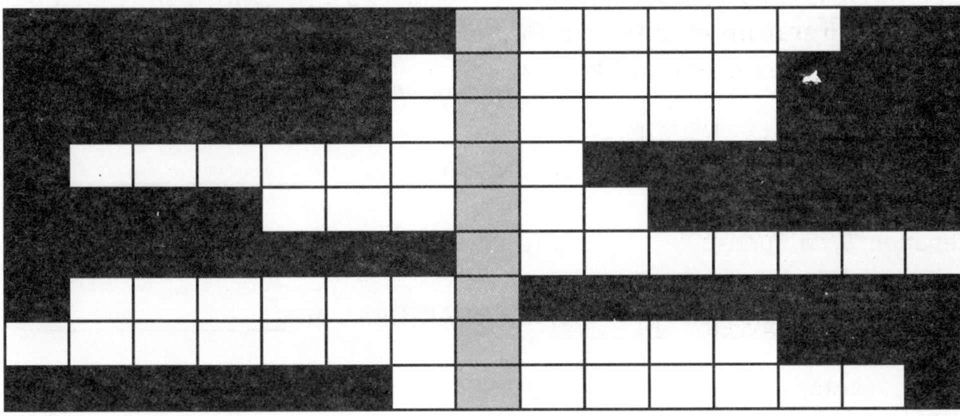

1. Damavand, Iran
2. Fansipan, Vietnam
3. Lhotse, Tibet
4. Kanchenjunga, India
5. Kinabalu, Malaysia
6. Makalu, border of China and Nepal
7. Noshaq, Afghanistan
8. Ramelau, East Timor
9. Yushan, Taiwan

Asian volcano: — — — — — — — — —

ASIA

14. RIVERS OF DELIGHT

Unscramble the names of these Asian rivers in the second column. The countries through which they flow are given as clues.

Country/ies	**Scrambled-up river**	**Correct name**
Myanmar	a. WARDIRADY	i. ____________________
China	b. ZENGYAT	ii. ____________________
Lebanon, Syria, Turkey	c. TORSOEN	iii. ____________________
China, India, Bangladesh	d. HARMPARTUBA	iv. ____________________
China, Pakistan	e. DUINS	v. ____________________
Thailand, Vietnam, Cambodia	f. GOMENK	vi. ____________________
Afghanistan, Tajikistan	g. MAU YARAD	vii. ____________________
Turkey, Syria, Iraq	h. TEUSHARPE	viii. ____________________

15. LEADING FROM THE FRONT

Match the names of the political leaders with the countries they led.

	Political Leader		Country
1.	Mao Zedong	a.	The Philippines
2.	Jawaharlal Nehru	b.	North Korea
3.	Saddam Hussein	c.	Pakistan
4.	Aung San Suu Kyi	d.	South Korea
5.	Benjamin Netanyahu	e.	Palestine
6.	Shinzo Abe	f.	Israel
7.	Yasser Arafat	g.	India
8.	Recep Tayyip Erdoğan	h.	Myanmar
9.	Kim Jong-il	i.	Iraq
10.	Benigno Aquino III	j.	China
11.	Mohammed Ali Jinnah	k.	Japan
12.	Park Geun-hye	l.	Turkey

16. LUSCIOUS LANGUAGES

Each set of letters below has the names of two Asian languages mixed up. Can you identify them? As a clue, you are given the name of a city in each of the countries. The first letter is the first letter of the first language, and the second letter is the first letter of the second language.

1. A B R U A R B M I E S C E (Jeddah, Mandalay)
2. G H E O E R B G R I E A W N (Batumi, Beersheba)
3. J K A H P A M N E E R S E (Yokohama, Sihanoukville)
4. M L A A L O A Y (Malacca City, Luang Prabang)
5. N P E A P S A H L T I O (Pokhara, Herat)
6. P P E O R R T U S G I U E A S N E (Isfahan, Macau)
7. S U I N Z H B A E L K A (Jaffna, Samarkand)
8. K F U I R L I D P I I N S O H (Mosul, Quezon City)
9. C D A Z N O T N O G N K E H S A E (Hong Kong, Paro)
10. U D R A D R U I (Karachi, Kandahar)

ASIA

17. COMFORT FOOD

The name of each Asian dish in the first column contains a word that fits the clue given in the second column. To find this word, cross off the extra letters in the name of the dish and read the remaining letters from left to right. The country to which this dish belongs is given in brackets.

Dish	**Clue**	**Answer**
EXAMPLE:		
S ~~H A K S H~~ O U K ~~A~~ (Israel)	**An Arab word for market**	**SOUK**
1. Garudhiya (Maldives)	It used to mean 'happy'	________
2. Motabel (Qatar)	An out-of-control group of people	________
3. Murtabak (Brunei)	Another word for bill in a restaurant	________
4. Machboos (Kuwait)	The sound made by a cow	________
5. Besbarmak (Kazakhstan)	What a bird uses to pick up food	________
6. Lumpia (Philippines)	A referee, in short	________
7. Popoki Muraba (Armenia)	Transfer from a jug to a glass	________
8. Biryani (India)	What you do in a race, past tense	________
9. Nasi Padang (Indonesia)	Accompanied music with your voice	________
10. Ramen (Japan)	Word said at the end of a prayer	________

ASIA

18. WRITING IT UP

Hidden in the grid are the names of 10 Asian language scripts. Strike off the names vertically, horizontally and diagonally.

D	Y	N	C	I	A	M	A	R	A
E	E	K	A	L	P	L	M	G	Q
S	C	V	D	I	D	P	U	N	T
E	Y	T	A	R	G	R	J	I	B
N	R	I	N	N	M	R	B	N	C
I	I	M	D	U	A	E	O	I	V
L	L	D	K	D	T	G	B	E	K
A	K	H	K	A	I	A	A	A	G
B	I	T	N	D	R	S	N	R	D
R	C	P	N	A	Y	A	H	V	I

ASIA

19. MOVIE MAGIC

Choose one letter from the box, given below, and fill it into the blanks such that the words form the name of a movie made by a famous film director. The name of the director is mentioned alongside.

A	B	C	D	G	H	I	K	L	M	M
N	O	R	S	U	V	W	X	Y	Z	

1. S _ A _ AMVARAM (Adoor Gopalakrishnan)
2. SE _ EN SA _ URAI (Akira Kurosawa)
3. _ HARU _ ATA (Satyajit Ray)
4. C _ UNGKING E _ PRESS (Wong Kar-Wai)
5. U _ ETS _ (Kenji Mizoguchi)
6. SALL _ H SHA _ ATI (Ephraim Kishon)
7. WOR _ ING G _ RLS I (Ishmael Bernal)
8. B _ L (Shoaib Mansoor)
9. _ UKTIR GAA _ (Tareque Masud)
10. A _ IME TO LIVE, A TIME TO _ IE (Hou Hsaio-Hsien)
11. WHERE I _ THE _ RIEND'S HOME? (Abbas Kiarostami)

ASIA

20. WORDS TO LIVE BY

Unscramble the words given below to read a quote by the Dalai Lama.

EW ANC REENV TONBAI ACEPE NI

__ ___ _____ ______ _____ __

HET ROUTE DROWL

___ _____ _____

NILUT EW KEMA CAPEE

_____ __ ____ _____

HITW SOLEURSEV.

____ _________

21. WHERE AM I?

Find the African countries hidden in the following sentences:

1. Listen, Ma, law is the only thing I want to study.
2. Is this bacon going bad?
3. He knows how to juggle so thoroughly that we get tired of waiting for him to drop something.
4. I'll take this rug and a footstool, please.
5. I gather it reassures you to see me study for my exams?
6. We have special geriatric facilities at this gym.
7. The coach addressed the team before the Olympic final.
8. I got this vibe nine days ago that something's up with the management.
9. I want to go to Africa.
10. Slender, wan damsel, a sip of this magic potion will restore you.

AFRICA

22. MUDDLED RIVERS

The names of rivers and the country in which they originate have been mixed together in the correct order. The first letter is the first letter in the name of the river and the name of the country starts with the second letter. Fill in the blanks correctly.

1. L S I O U T M H A P F R O I C P O A

   River: ______________ Country of origin: ______________

2. O L R E S A O N T H G O E

   River: ______________ Country of origin: ______________

3. Z Z A M A B M B I E Z A I

   River: ______________ Country of origin: ______________

4. O A K N A G V O A L N G A O

   River: ______________ Country of origin: ______________

5. S G E U N I E N G E A L A

   River: ______________ Country of origin: ______________

6. V G O H L A N T A A

   River: ______________ Country of origin: ______________

7. N G U I I N G E E R A

   River: ______________ Country of origin: ______________

8. B E L T U H I E O N P I L I E A

   River: ______________ Country of origin: ______________

23. ADDING LANGUAGES

The names of 12 African languages have been broken up into two groups. Match a letter group in Column A with another one in Column B to complete the name of an African language.

Column A	Column B
1. HAU	a. BO
2. BER	b. LU
3. NUB	c. SA
4. MAA	d. GASY
5. YOR	e. BELE
6. ASH	f. SA
7. IG	g. ANTI
8. KIR	h. IAN
9. MALA	i. UBA
10. XHO	j. BER
11. ZU	k. UNDI
12. NDE	l. SAI

AFRICA

24. PARK IT HERE

The name of each African national park or game reserve in the first column below contains a word that fits the clue given in that line. To find this word, cross off the extra letters in the national park's name and read the remaining letters from left to right. The country where this national park or game reserve is located is given in brackets.

EXAMPLE: A ~~M~~ B ~~O~~ S ~~E~~ ~~L~~ ~~I~~ (Kenya)

The six-pack you want on your body = ABS

National Park	Clue	Answer
Bwindi (Uganda)	You throw trash in it	________
Chobe (Botswana)	A gardening tool	________
Hwange (Zimbabwe)	What the dog does with its tail	________
Lake Nakuru (Kenya)	When a tap drips	________
Sabi Sands (South Africa)	A group of musicians	________
Ngorongoro (Tanzania)	Midday	________
South Luangwa (Zambia)	When ice melts	________
Namib-Naukluft (Namibia)	Type of luxury fur coat	________

AFRICA

25. A BIRD BY ANOTHER NAME

Unscramble the bird names below to identify the national birds of various African countries.

Country **Scrambled Version** **National Bird**

1. Egypt DONGLE GALEE _ _ _ _ _ _ _ _ _ _ _

2. Liberia NARDEG LUBBLU _ _ _ _ _ _ _ _ _ _ _ _

3. Cape Verde YGRE-ADDEEH FIRESHINKG _

4. Mauritius OODD _ _ _ _

5. Sudan STEARYCER RIBD _ _ _ _ _ _ _ _ _ _ _ _ _ _

6. Malawi CAFINAR SHIF GALEE _ _ _ _ _ _ _ _ _ _ _ _ _ _ _ _ _

7. South Africa LEBU NACRE _ _ _ _ _ _ _ _ _

8. Angola EDR-CSTEEDR RUCOAT _ _ _-_ _ _ _ _ _ _ _ _ _ _ _ _ _

9. Cote d'Ivoire THEWI-HECKEED AROCUT _ _ _ _ _-_ _ _ _ _ _ _ _ _ _ _ _ _ _

10. Nigeria CBALK-RENDCOW ERNAC _ _ _ _ _-_ _ _ _ _ _ _ _ _ _ _ _ _

11. Swaziland LUPPER-DETERSC ACORUT _ _ _ _ _ _ _-_ _ _ _ _ _ _ _ _ _ _ _ _ _

12. Botswana CALLI-DBEATERS RRELLO _ _ _ _ _ _-_ _ _ _ _ _ _ _ _ _ _ _ _ _ _

The **African fish eagle** is the national bird of four African countries listed below. Fill one letter in each blank to find the answers. All the **A**s have been filled in to help you.

_ A _ _ _ _ A , _ _ _ _ _ _ _ _ A _ , _ A _ _ _ A, _ _ _ _ A _ _ _

26. ANIMALS ACROSS AFRICA

Given below are clues to the names of some unusual African animals. Solve the clues to fill in the crossword.

Across:

1. This almost extinct small animal with scales covering its body folds up into the shape of a football when it encounters danger. It uses its long, sticky tongue to catch ants.
7. The fastest animal on land, it cannot climb tall trees.
8. It uses its long, sticky tongue to feed on ants and termites.

10. The largest rodent in Africa, this herbivorous animal has a natural means of defence. Contrary to belief it doesn't use its spikes to attack other animals.

11. The most reclusive of the big cats, this animal is one of the Big Five that people like to view on safaris.

13. This animal is also known as bushbaby because It cries like a child in distress when in danger.

Down:

2. A species of lemur in Madagascar, this nocturnal animal that feeds on insect larvae, has large eyes and ears and is often killed on sight because it is considered to be a bad omen.

3. This largest living primate is a shy vegetarian.

4. Africa's largest living reptile.

5. This Madagascar origin nocturnal animal was mistaken for a ghost in ancient times because of its bright shining eyes and grey fur on a black and white tail.

6. An animal that looks like a rodent, but has a long nose, long tail and very long legs for its body.

9. A finless marine animal with paddling forelimbs and a whale-like tail. It is a distant cousin of the elephant.

10. This animal found only in cold polar climates has a small colony in South Africa due to the cold water currents.

12. The largest bird in the world.

27. PRECIOUS RESERVES

The countries listed below have reserves of a rare mineral. Insert the country names into the grid and read the shaded column top down to find out which mineral it is.

Algeria	Central African Republic		Gabon
Malawi	Namibia	South Africa	Zambia

28. MINER-AL-PHABET

Choose one letter from the pool of letters in the box to fill in the blanks such that the words form the name of a mineral found in abundance in the country mentioned alongside.

A	B	C	D	E	F	G	H	I	K	L	M
N	O	P	R	S	T	U	V	W	X	Y	Z

1. BAU _ ITE, Guinea
2. CO _ ALT, Democratic Republic of Congo
3. C _ ROMITE, Madagascar
4. MAN _ ANESE, Gabon
5. U _ ANIUM, Niger
6. GOL _ , Burkina Faso
7. NIC _ EL, Tanzania
8. PETROL _ UM, Libya
9. G _ PSUM, Somalia
10. PHO _ PHORITE, Tunisia
11. _ ANADIUM, South Africa
12. T _ NGSTEN, South Sudan
13. DIAM _ NDS, Botswana
14. _ OLFRAMITE, Rwanda
15. TAL _, Egypt
16. TITA _ IUM ORE, Sierra Leone
17. A _ UMINIUM, Mozambique
18. PLA _ INUM, Burundi
19. COP _ ER, Zambia
20. _ SBESTOS, Swaziland
21. LITHIU _, Zimbabwe
22. _ LUORITE, Kenya
23. _ INC, Bolivia
24. _ RON ORE, Mauritania

AFRICA

29. CAPITAL FRAGMENTS

Bits and pieces of 20 African capitals appear below. Can you identify each one just by the letters that are given (one capital is identified for you)? Remember that some capitals have two-word names.

1. DIS – MogaDIShu, Somalia
2. JUM – ____________
3. NAN – ____________
4. IGA – ____________
5. UNI – ____________
6. ABA – ____________
7. APU – ____________
8. ODO – ____________
9. UBA – ____________
10. UAN – ____________
11. BRE – ____________
12. DHO – ____________
13. RAI – ____________
14. ROV – ____________
15. CRA – ____________
16. RTL – ____________
17. OUG – ____________
18. PAL – ____________
19. CTO – ____________
20. SAB – ____________

30. WHO AM I?

Use the clues, given below, to identify these African countries.

1. The youngest country in Africa – S _ _ _ _   S _ _ _ _
2. The Victoria Falls, one of the seven wonders of the world, are located in this former British colony – Z _ _ _ _ _
3. Nicknamed "The Warm Heart of Africa", this is one of the smallest countries of the continent. About one-third of area is taken up by a large lake – M _ _ _ _ _
4. The dictator Idi Amin staged a military coup in 1971 to head this country – U _ _ _ _ _
5. It is called the "Land of a Thousand Hills" because of its green, mountainous landscape, and boasts the renowned Volcanoes National Park – R _ _ _ _ _
6. It is the only independent country in the world which lies entirely above 1000 metres above sea level – L _ _ _ _ _ _

31. RENAMED

Match the names of African countries in Column A with the names they were known by in the past in Column B.

Present Name	**Earlier Name**
1. Zambia	a. Basutoland
2. Malawi	b. German South-West Africa
3. Zimbabwe	c. Ubangi-Shari
4. Djibouti	d. Bechuanaland
5. Botswana	e. Nyasaland
6. Lesotho	f. Sudanese Republic
7. Benin	g. Northern Rhodesia
8. Mali	h. Malagasy Republic
9. Ghana	i. Southern Rhodesia
10. Central African Republic	j. French Somaliland
11. Democratic Republic of the Congo	k. Grain Coast
12. Burkina Faso	l. Zaire
13. Liberia	m. Dahomey
14. Namibia	n. Gold Coast
15. Madagascar	o. Upper Volta

32. MYSTERY ISLE

Use the clues given below to identify various African island nations.

1. This African country is the only member of the Arab League that is completely in the Southern Hemisphere.
2. This country is a biodiversity hotspot. Over 90 per cent of its wildlife is found nowhere else on earth.
3. This country was uninhabited before the arrival of the Portuguese around 1470 AD.
4. This is the smallest country in Africa.
5. This country spans an archipelago of 10 volcanic islands.
6. This country was an important trade route from Europe to the east before the opening of the Suez Canal. It was also involved in the power struggle between the French and the British.

33. CURRENCY ISSUES

Join two letter groups from the box below to find the currency of various African countries.

KWA	UIYA	LO	LA	DI	RA
ESC	RR	RA	TI	NGENI	ARIARY
ASI	PU	DAL	OUG	UDO	RA
NAI	LILA	NZA	FA	MET	NAK
MALAGASY	ND	CE	ICAL	DOB	BI

1. Angola – ____________________
2. Mauritania – ____________________
3. Swaziland – ____________________
4. São Tomé and Príncipe – ____________________
5. Ghana – ____________________
6. Nigeria – ____________________
7. Ethiopia – ____________________
8. Botswana – ____________________
9. Eritrea – ____________________
10. Madagascar – ____________________
11. South Africa – ____________________
12. Lesotho – ____________________
13. Mozambique – ____________________
14. Cape Verde – ____________________
15. Gambia – ____________________

34. AFRICAN ADVENTURES

Add the missing consonants to identify famous novels written in English and set in Africa. The author's name is an additional clue.

1. H Rider Haggard – _ I _ _   _ O _ O _ O _'_   _ I _ E _
2. Joseph Conrad – _ EA _ _   O_   _ A _ _ _ E _ _
3. Edgar Rice Burroughs – _ A _ _ A N   O_   _ _ E   A_ E _
4. Hugh Lofting – _ _ E   _ _ O _ _   O_   _ O _ _ O _   _ O _ I _ _ _ E
5. Jules Verne – _ I _ E   _ E E _ _   I _   A   _ A _ _ O O _
6. Wilbur Smith – E _ E _ _ A _ _   _ O _ _
7. R M Ballantyne – _ _ E   _ O _ I _ _ A   _ U _ _ E _ _
8. Frederick Forsyth – _ _ E   _ O _ _   O _   _ A _
9. James Patterson – _ _ O _ _   _ O U _ _ _ _
10. Desmond Bagley – _ U _ _ E _ _ A U _

AFRICA

35. PEACE BE TO ALL!

Unscramble the names of the Nobel Peace Prize winners from various African countries.

	Country	Scrambled Version	Winner, Nobel Peace Prize
1.	Egypt	RAWAN LE DASTA	____________
2.	South Africa	EMODDNS UUTT	____________
3.	Liberia	EELNL SONNOJH LIFERSA	____________
4.	South Africa	SENNOL LAMENAD	____________
5.	Kenya	GRAINWA TAUM HAMATAI	____________
6.	Egypt	DAHEMMO DRABAILEE	____________
7.	Liberia	HALEMY WEBOGE	____________

AFRICA

36. JUST DESERTS

Thirteen African deserts are hidden in the grid below. Read diagonally, vertically, horizontally, upwards and backwards to find them. Answers may overlap.

A	B	A	B	A	N	E	D	A	G	O	O	R	A	K	N
R	A	V	I	Y	I	L	P	R	F	Y	B	E	B	A	R
A	L	B	I	S	Y	F	L	A	L	E	A	L	M	L	T
B	I	R	S	H	T	U	M	H	O	L	I	I	L	A	E
D	I	T	O	N	O	R	A	A	W	I	B	L	A	H	C
N	R	H	A	P	H	R	T	S	S	M	R	A	N	A	T
A	G	B	M	O	C	A	M	E	D	E	S	B	O	R	C
R	U	O	L	A	V	A	B	O	D	A	N	A	K	I	L
G	L	A	T	S	A	O	C	N	A	E	R	T	I	R	E

AFRICA

37. DANCING THE NIGHT AWAY

Join together two separate word sections from the three-letter groups below to make six-letter words that answers each clue. Write the word in the grid going downward. Each three-letter piece is used only once, so you can cross it off. When the grid is complete, read across the shaded rows to find the names of the national dance of the Democratic Republic of Congo and Ethiopia.

UST	INK	OUS	UNJ	ANS	SAL	SES
ORG	KOU	AME	IVA	ODI	UPL	ROI

1	2	3	4	5	6	7
S						
E						
S						
A						
M						
E						

Clues:

1. One of the words Ali Baba said to open the door of the cave filled with treasure.
2. Repugnant or disgusting.
3. How to transmit data from an earth station to a communications satellite.
4. Antique sculptures of young men.
5. The collective name for stomach, lungs, brain, liver, spleen etc.
6. Not fair.
7. Spittle

The national dance of the Democratic Republic of the Congo (top row) – ____________________.

The national dance of Ethiopia (bottom row) – ____________________.

38. JUST LIKE AN EGYPTIAN

How much do you know about ancient Egypt? Find out by using the clues given below to fill in the blanks.

1. The common title for the kings of Ancient Egypt – P _ _ _ _ _ _
2. A giant tomb built for the kings of Ancient Egypt – _ _ _ _ _ _ _
3. This plant grew on the banks of the Nile River and was used to make paper – _ _ _ _ _ _ _
4. A person especially trained to read and write – _ _ _ _ _ _
5. A tall pillar monument generally built in pairs near the entrances of ancient Egyptian temples – _ _ _ _ _ _ _
6. A type of ancient Egyptian writing – _ _ _ _ _ _ _ _ _ _
7. A mythological beast with the body of a lion and the head of a god – _ _ _ _ _ _
8. This object symbolised the beetle, which was considered holy – _ _ _ _ _ _
9. This ancient Egyptian character resembles the Christian cross, and is known as the "breath of life" or the key of the Nile – _ _ _ _
10. A dead body that has been preserved by embalming so that it will not rot – _ _ _ _ _

AFRICA

39. FAMOUS SAYINGS

Solve the clues and fill one letter in each blank. Then insert the letters according to the numbers given below into the sentence to find a saying by a famous African leader.

The first part of the day: M O R N I N G
1 2 3 4 5 4 6

You go to school to do this: _ _ _ _ _
7 8 9 10 11

The past tense of what a bird does: _ _ _ _
12 13 14 15

A book is divided into many of these: _ _ _ _ _ _ _ _
16 17 18 19 8 14 3 7

_ _ _ _ _ _ _ O _   _ _   _ _ _   _ O _ _
14 10 9 16 18 8 5 2 4   5 7   8 17 14   1 2 7 8

_ O _ _ _ _ _ _
19 2 15 14 3 12 9 13

_ _ _ _ O _   _ _ _ _ _   _ O _   _ _ _
15 14 18 19 2 4   15 17 5 16 17   11 2 9   16 18 4

_ _ _   _ O
9 7 14   8 2

_ _ _ _ _ _   _ _ _   _ O _ _ _. - N _ _ _ O _
16 17 18 4 6 14   8 17 14   15 2 3 13 10   4 14 13 7 2 4

_ _ _ _ _ _ _
1 18 4 10 14 13 18

40. GEOGRAPHICAL ODDITIES

Given below are the names of some African countries. One country in each group is the odd one out because of its geography. Which one is it, and why does it not belong to the group?

1. Eritrea, Gabon, Djibouti, Somalia, Ethiopia
2. Senegal, Morocco, Algeria, Tunisia
3. Kenya, Tanzania, Rwanda, Burundi, Namibia
4. Zambia, Namibia, Botswana, South Africa, Mozambique
5. Botswana, Namibia, Kenya, South Africa
6. Angola, Nigeria, Benin, Cote d'Ivoire, Cameroon
7. Mali, Niger, Chad, Sudan, Sierra Leone
8. Angola, Namibia, Central African Republic, South Africa, Mozambique
9. Congo Republic, Somalia, Democratic Republic of the Congo, Tanzania, Burundi
10. Mali, Algeria, Libya, Cameroon, Egypt

41. COUNTRIFIED

Some countries that make up Oceania are hidden in the sentences below. Find them.

1. The sufi jiggled his bowl of coins to show he wanted alms.
2. It was the first time the doctor had heard the contessa moan with pain.
3. I've never heard of a tutu valued at one thousand dollars before now.
4. Athletes from France, China, Uruguay and Zambia were led to the fourth floor of the hotel.
5. Some guy trying to act too smart for his own good called his new t-shirt designs "Harakiri Batiked".
6. We're walking on eggshells because the principal auditor is expected today.
7. The skeleton gallery was the scariest place in the biology museum.

42. CAPITAL GAME

Given below is a list of countries. Match the countries with their correct capital.

Country

1. Nauru
2. Papua New Guinea
3. Samoa
4. Marshall Islands
5. Kiribati
6. Tonga
7. Vanuatu
8. Solomon Islands
9. Micronesia
10. Palau
11. Fiji
12. Tuvalu
13. New Zealand
14. Australia

Capital

a. South Tarawa
b. Port Vila
c. Wellington
d. Honiara
e. Canberra
f. Palikir
g. Funafuti
h. Suva
i. Majuro
j. Nuku'alofa
k. Port Moresby
l. Apia
m. Yaren District
n. Ngerulmud

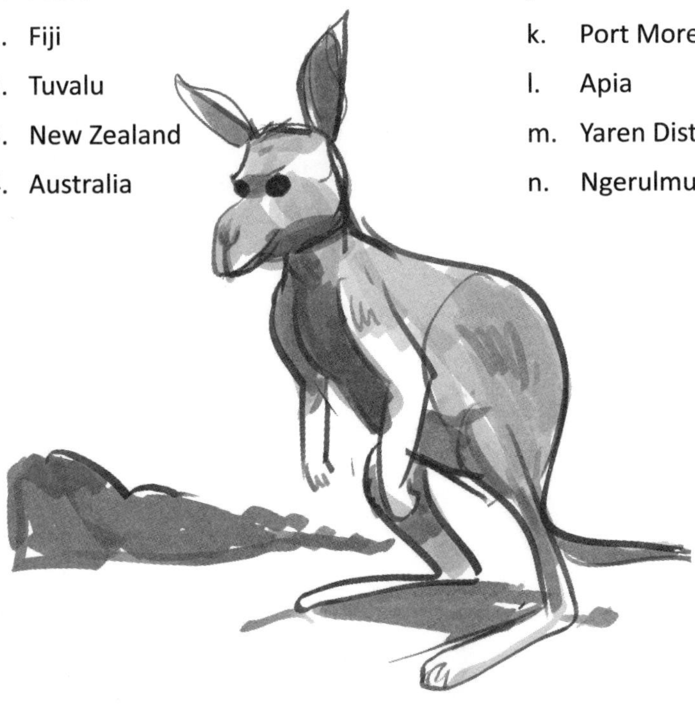

43. POCKETING THE MARSUPIALS

Marsupials are mammals whose young are born incompletely developed and are carried and suckled in a pouch on the mother's belly. Arrange the marsupials listed below, in the grid and read down the shaded column to find the names of the national animal and national bird of Australia.

ANTECHINUS, BANDICOOT, BETTONG, GLIDER, KOALA, MULGARA, NUMBAT, PADEMELON, QUOKKA, QUOLL, TASMANIAN DEVIL, WALLABY, WALLAROO, WOYLIE

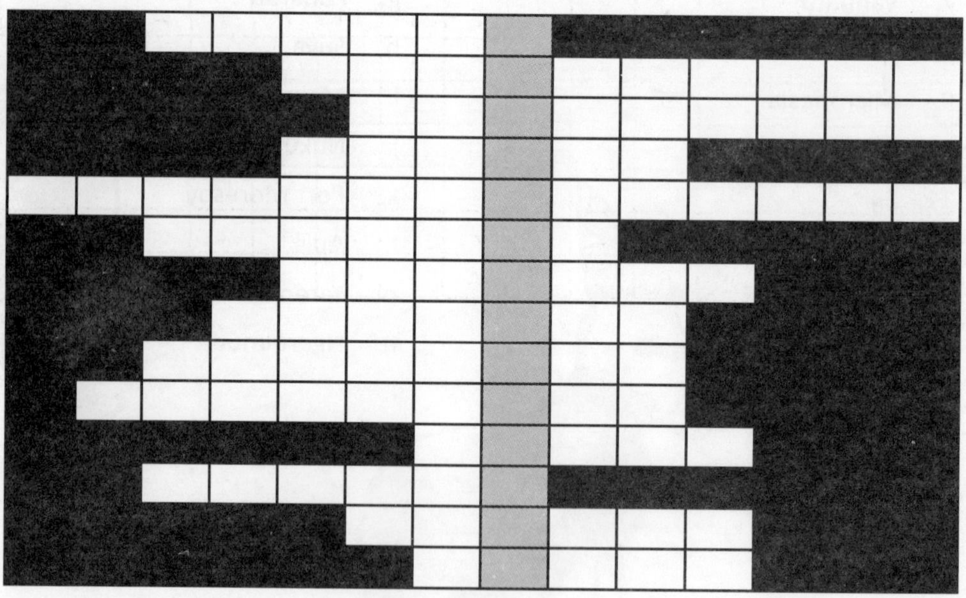

44. IT DEPENDS

Hidden in the grid are the names of 10 dependent territories of Oceania. Strike off the names vertically, horizontally and diagonally.

F	R	E	N	C	H	P	O	L	Y	N	E	S	I	A
G	N	O	R	F	O	L	K	I	S	L	A	N	D	N
J	U	Z	A	S	P	R	F	T	G	I	V	B	Z	U
G	A	A	O	T	R	W	S	E	N	A	E	V	A	T
K	T	L	M	R	E	E	E	O	Q	U	O	L	R	U
K	W	A	A	E	L	A	D	R	O	T	E	Y	R	F
Y	R	M	S	W	T	E	O	L	O	K	U	I	U	D
H	T	P	N	D	L	D	U	N	O	S	P	R	Y	N
I	H	S	A	A	F	G	F	T	M	F	Y	A	N	A
P	I	T	C	A	I	R	N	I	S	L	A	N	D	S
I	H	W	I	P	E	P	L	A	T	E	R	E	S	I
I	E	T	R	A	Q	U	D	E	D	W	S	T	Y	L
N	F	K	E	E	I	E	I	U	O	M	M	K	J	L
I	R	T	M	P	L	T	X	N	A	I	E	E	W	A
E	P	S	A	R	D	N	A	L	S	I	E	K	A	W

45. PEEK-A-BOO!

Each three-letter group given below is contained in the name of a city in Australia or New Zealand. Can you identify these cities?

3-letter group	City
EXAMPLE:	
ELH	**DELHI**
1. ART	____________
2. IRN	____________
3. ERT	____________
4. ISB	____________
5. ARW	____________
6. LLA	____________
7. ELA	____________
8. DNE	____________
9. OUR	____________
10. ERR	____________
11. EDI	____________
12. UCK	____________
13. TCH	____________
14. ING	____________
15. ARG	____________

46. (F)ANTARCTIC ANIMALS

Given below are the names of some animals found in Antarctica. Rearrange the letters to find the name of each animal.

UBEL-DEEY GASH ____________________

MORPEER GENUINP ____________________

ANGTI LEPTER ____________________

PAROLED ALES ____________________

TRACEBARE SLAE ____________________

LILRK ____________________

TRICCA RENT ____________________

ACEP NOPEGI ____________________

NYWSO STILEBLAHH ____________________

OWNS EELPTR ____________________

CANTACRIT AUSK ____________________

HOSTERNU URF ASLE ____________________

GINK GINPENU ____________________

GRANDWINE BRATASLOS ____________________

47. ATTENTION, FILM-GOERS!

Each clue below hints at a film personality from Oceania. Fill one letter in each blank to find out who the film celebrity is.

1. Lead actor in *A Beautiful Mind* – _ _ _ _ _ _ _ _ _ _ _ _ _
2. Lead actress in *The Lord of the Rings: The Return of the King* – _ _ _ _ _ _ _ _ _ _ _ _ _ _
3. Lead actress in *Xena: Warrior Princess* – _ _ _ _ _ _ _ _ _ _ _ _
4. Lead actor in *Avatar* – _ _ _ _ _ _ _ _ _ _ _ _ _
5. Lead actress in *The Ring* – _ _ _ _ _ _ _ _ _ _
6. Lead actor in *Pirates of the Caribbean: Curse of the Black Pearl* – _ _ _ _ _ _ _ _ _ _ _ _ _
7. Lead actress in *Batman Forever* – _ _ _ _ _ _ _ _ _ _ _ _
8. Lead actress in *Finding Neverland* – _ _ _ _ _ _ _ _ _ _ _ _ _ _
9. Lead actor in *X-Men* – _ _ _ _ _ _ _ _ _ _ _
10. Lead actor in *The Dark Knight* – _ _ _ _ _ _ _ _ _ _ _

48. OCCUPATIONAL HAZARD

Given below is a list of achievers from Oceania. Match them with the field in which they have excelled.

Achievers	**Field of excellence**
1. Sir Donald Bradman	a. Screenwriter, producer, director
2. Ernest Rutherford	b. Golfer
3. Ngaio Marsh	c. Rugby player
4. Margaret Court	d. Inventor
5. Jane Campion	e. Chef
6. Sir Edmund Hillary	f. Novelist
7. Bruce McLaren	g. Innovator, founder – Royal Flying Doctor Service
8. Greg Norman	h. Cricketer
9. Gina Rinehart	i. Fashion designer
10. Stephen Peter Kearney	j. Mountaineer
11. David Warren	k. Nobel prize-winning chemist
12. Kate Sheppard	l. Tennis player
13. Curtis Stone	m. Suffragette
14. Alex Perry	n. Race car driver
15. Rev John Flynn	o. Businessperson

49. BOOK IT!

Choose one letter from the letters given below and fill it into the blanks such that the words form the name of a Booker prize-winning author from Oceania. The name of the book for which s/he won the prize is mentioned alongside.

A	C	F	G	H	K	L	N	P	T	Y

1.	THOMAS _ E _ EALLY	*Schindler's Ark*
2.	KERI _ U _ ME	*The Bone People*
3.	PETER _ ARE _	*Oscar and Lucinda, True History of the Kelly Gang*
4.	DBC _ IERRE	*Vernon God Little*
5.	ELEANOR C _ T _ ON	*The Luminaries*
6.	RICHARD _ LANA _ AN	*The Narrow Road to the Deep North*

50. QUIET FLOWS THE RIVER

The names of 12 rivers have been broken up in three letter-groups. Match a letter group in Column A with letters in Columns B and C to complete the name of a river in Oceania.

	A	B	C	River
1.	DRE	WE	Y	___________
2.	PA	L	DGEE	___________
3.	KAB	LI	AY	___________
4.	MU	REN	TO	___________
5.	AV	EN	NOO	___________
6.	MURR	KA	A	___________
7.	DAR	VU	CE	___________
8.	WAI	KE	NG	___________
9.	CLA	UMBI	AU	___________
10.	DER	RR	TI	___________
11.	NA	PE	NT	___________
12.	F	AN	A	___________

51. HERITAGE BOX

Join three letter groups from the box below to make the names of famous heritage sites from Oceania. Write the correct name against the clues given.

island	rier reef	bikini	erson	mata	uka
east	rock	fraser	pounamu	bay	phoenix
riro	roi	great Bar	lev	island	hend
Islands	shark	tonga	rennel	atoll	Te Wahi
Kuk	Swamp				

1. It is the largest area of seagrass meadows in the world and a critical habitat for endangered dugongs (Australia) – ______________
2. It features uninhabited limestone islands of volcanic origin and has the highest concentration of marine lakes separated from the ocean by land barriers (Palau) – ______________
3. It provides evidence of primitive irrigation and cultivation systems from about 9000 years ago (Papua New Guinea) – ______________
4. The world's largest raised coral atoll, a part of which surrounds its former lagoon, which is now the largest lake in the Pacific Ocean. (Solomon Islands) – ______________
5. It hosts an outstanding level of marine biodiversity and is the world's largest coral reef system. (Australia) – ______________
6. 67 nuclear weapons tests were conducted here by the United States between 1946 and 1958. The site contains many visible remains of the effects of nuclear testing. (Marshall Islands) – ______________
7. The world's largest sand island, it is the only place where tall rainforest grows on sand. (Australia) – ______________

8. Renowned for its geological and cultural significance, many of its summits are sacred to the Maori. (New Zealand) – ______________

9. The domain of a 13th century chief whose social reforms continue to be relevant to local society, it consists of his residence, the site of his death, and his burial site. (Vanuatu) – ______________

10. This mountainous landscape of ridges and fords shaped by thousands of years of glacial excavation hosts the best surviving illustration of ancient Gondwanan wildlife, much of which is rare and unique to the area. (New Zealand) – ______________

11. One of the most remote islands in the world, its ecosystem hosts multiple endemic species and is undisturbed by human activity, providing the opportunity to study the dynamics of an isolated ecosystem. (Pitcairn Islands) – ______________

12. The first European settlement in Fiji, the many well-preserved buildings of the era make it an excellent example of a colonial port developed during the late 19th century in the South Pacific. (Fiji) – ______________

13. It is sparsely inhabited, inhospitable and protects one of the world's largest oceanic wildnernesses, thereby helping evaluate the consequences of climate change on sea levels (Kiribati) – ______________

52. IDENTITY CRISIS

Each set of letters here has the names of two cricketers mixed up. Can you identify them? The first two letters are the first letters in the names of the first and second cricketers, respectively.

1. A B R D E N A D M A N M G C C I U L L C H L R U I S M T
2. R D I E C N H N A R I D S H L A D I L L L E E E E
3. R R I O C K S Y S P T O A N Y T L I O N R G
4. S H D A A N V E I D W W A A R R N N E E R
5. M M A I C R H A T I E N L G C U L P A T R I K L E L
6. G B L E N R N M E C G T R T A L T E H E
7. B A R D A A D M M H I L O L G E G R
8. M D A A R N K I G E I L L L V E E T S T P O I R E I
9. M C I A C M E H A R E O L N H W U H S I S T E E Y
10. S M T A E R V K E T W A A Y U L G O H R

53. CAN-BERRA?

In 1912, the Australian Government invited suggestions from the public for the name of the capital city. It was eventually called Canberra, but if you arrange the cities in the grid and read down the shaded column, you will find one of the more outlandish suggestions.

WALLA WALLA, WANGARATTA, WARMUN, WAROOKA, WAROONA, WESTONIA, WHYALLA, WILMOT, WOMBEYAN CAVES, WONTHAGGI, WOOLI, WUDINNA, WYONG

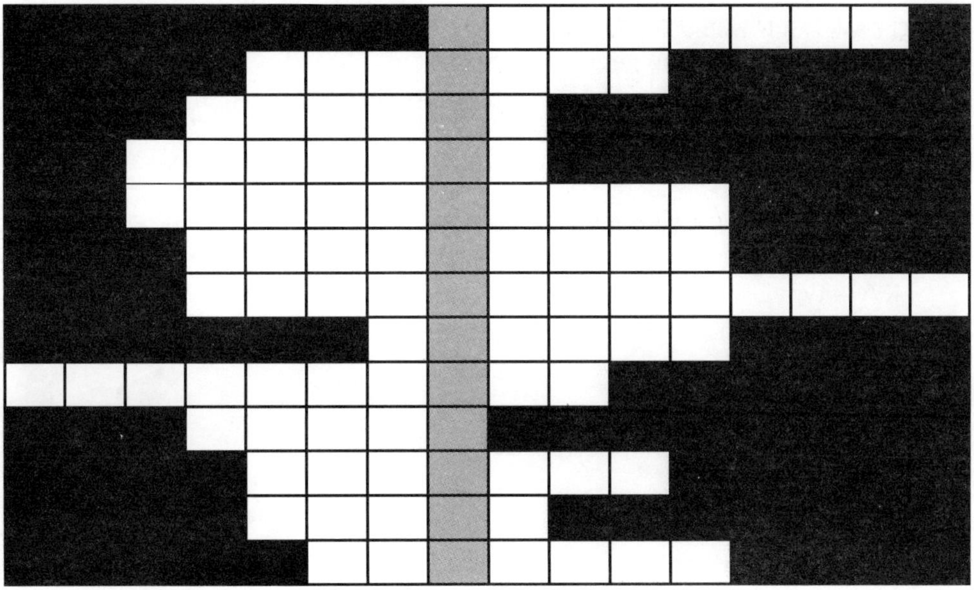

54. MAORI CULTURE

In each pair of puzzles, the first three letters are the same. Solve them to find the three letters, and then put them in the second word to find the name of an essential element of Maori culture.

EXAMPLE

T E R M S (the school year is divided into this)
T E R E O (Maori language)

_ _ _ O R A S (a snack of vegetables covered in spiced gram flour and fried)
_ _ _ E H A (Maori term for people of European descent)

_ _ _ K S (the numbers you get on a test or exam)
_ _ _ A E (the meeting place of Maori communities)

_ _ _ G O (India's national fruit)
_ _ _ A A K I T A N G A (hospitality and kindness)

_ _ _ K A (a type of noodles popular in India)
_ _ _ A (the traditional Maori war dance)

_ _ _ E R F U L (strong, mighty)
_ _ _ H I R I (the traditional Maori welcome ceremony)

_ _ _ L E (a very large mammal found in the ocean)
_ _ _ I K O R E R O (Maori oratory)

_ _ _ P A (What the letter 'K' is called in Greek)
_ _ _ A H A K A (Maori group performances)

_ _ _ E Y (bears like to eat this)
_ _ _ G I (the traditional Maori greeting)

55. FLYING OVER THE WATER

Fill in the blanks to form the names of birds. Then, read down the blanks to get the name of a water body that lies between Australia and New Zealand.

COCKA _ OO

R _ VEN

CA _ SOWARY

_ AGPIE

KOOK _ BURRA

HERO _

IBI _

LORIK _ ET

PL _ TYPUS

_ _ _ _ _ _ _ _ _ _ (water body)

56. LOST IN URBAN SPACES

Find the European cities hidden in the following sentences:

1. I could see the amber lining the walls of the palace.
2. The pupa risks being eaten by predators.
3. Eating teriyaki evokes memories of my time in Osaka.
4. I had no idea they were selling vitamin skin strips these days for better absorption of vitamins.
5. We lived in a neighbourhood of delinquents, so fiascos were a routine matter.
6. The discovery of odes saved me from falling into a depression.
7. An electrometer is an electrical instrument for measuring electric charge or electric potential difference.
8. His tan bulldog was the strangest animal I'd ever seen.
9. The watermelon donation camp was a wonderful way to combat heatstroke for the homeless.
10. We delayed our decision to buy a house in the hills when we saw the semi-landslide.

57. FRAGMENTED COAST

Each three-letter group given below is contained in the name of a European coastal city. The country to which this city belongs is given in brackets. Can you identify these cities?

3-letter group	**City**
Example: ERP (United Kingdom)	**LIVERPOOL**
1. INB (Scotland)	______________
2. ENI (Italy)	______________
3. STA (Turkey)	______________
4. SLO (Norway)	______________
5. ISB (Portugal)	______________
6. ELS (Finland)	______________
7. UBL (Ireland)	______________
8. ENH (Denmark)	______________
9. ELO (Spain)	______________
10. ROV (Croatia)	______________
11. ENO (Italy)	______________
12. SEI (France)	______________

58. MIXED BORDERS

Each set of letters here has the names of two European countries mixed up. Can you identify them? The first letter is the first letter of the first country, and the second letter is the first letter of the second country.

1. C B E Y L P A R R U U S S
2. P S A O N M R A T R U I G N A O L
3. A A N L D B O A N R I R A A
4. M M A O C N E T E D N O E G N R I O A
5. C S R W O E A D T E I N A
6. E G S R T E O E N C I E A
7. D G E E N R M M A A R N K Y
8. F L I I T N H L U A A N N I D A
9. A S R L O M V E A N K I I A A
10. K P O O L S A O N V D O
11. L N U E X T E H M E R B L O U A R N G D S
12. M M O A N L A T C A O

59. STARRING CITIES

Arrange the names of the cities listed below into the grid and read the shaded column top down to find out the name of a European country.

AYTOS, BURGAS, GABROVO, PERNIK, SHUMEN, TROYAN, VRATSA, YAMBOL

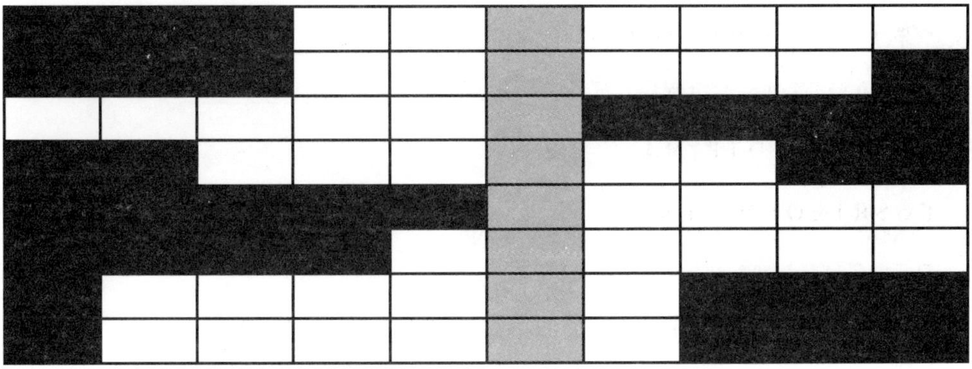

EUROPE

60. ADD CHEESE FOR FLAVOUR

The names of 15 cheeses have been broken up in three letter-groups. Match a letter group in Column A with letters in Columns B and C to complete the name of a European cheese.

	A	B	C	Cheese
1.	GR	MOL	DAR	________
2.	EM	EMB	TER	________
3.	FO	ILT	UE	________
4.	RA	MEN	TA	________
5.	RI	GON	RE	________
6.	CH	QUE	TI	________
7.	MAS	CL	PONE	________
8.	CAM	LLO	FORT	________
9.	ST	UYE	ON	________
10.	MU	ED	TAL	________
11.	RO	ND	ETTE	________
12.	HA	VAR	ZOLA	________
13.	HA	CAR	UMI	________
14.	MI	COT	ETTE	________
15.	GOR	NS	ERT	________

61. JUMBLED BRUSHES

Unscramble the names of European painters and match them with their works.

Name of Painting	**Painter**	**Unscrambled Name of Painter**
1. *The Card Players*	ALPU ANZNECE	________
2. *The Tilled Field*	ANJO OMIR	________
3. *The Yellow Christ*	UPLA UGGUNIA	________
4. *The Spanish Singer*	RADEUDO NATEM	________
5. *L'Absinthe*	GRADE SADGE	________
6. *Impression, Sunrise*	CAUDEL OTEMN	________
7. *Madonna and Child*	PARHELA	________
8. *The Disrobing of Christ*	LE CROEG	________
9. *The Last Judgment*	CLIMEHALEOGAN	________
10. *The Persistence of Memory*	DRAVOLSA IDAL	________

EUROPE

62. LOST IN THE MARKET

Hidden in the grid are the names of 15 European car brands. Strike off the names vertically, horizontally and diagonally.

MERCEDES	AUDI	PORSCHE	OPEL
BENTLEY	JAGUAR	VOLVO	DACIA
FIAT	FERRARI	PEUGEOT	CITROEN

J	M	M	T	A	I	F	J	T	G	M
P	E	U	G	E	O	T	F	I	A	T
T	N	S	E	D	E	C	R	E	M	P
B	I	E	Z	I	A	S	G	D	O	K
E	R	W	O	U	R	V	K	R	Q	A
N	A	A	D	R	O	A	S	O	I	D
T	R	I	U	L	T	C	R	C	D	O
L	R	T	V	G	H	I	A	R	P	A
E	E	O	D	E	A	D	C	E	E	L
Y	F	N	J	B	Z	J	L	K	K	F

63. PROTECT THE RIGHT ONE

Fifteen animals' names have been split into two columns. Can you match them correctly to identify some of the endangered animals of Europe?

First half of the animal name	**Second half of the animal name**
1. Karpathos	a. rock lizard
2. Iberian	b. pine vole
3. Apennine	c. pipistrelle
4. Carabo	d. minnow
5. Canary	e. mouse-tailed dormouse
6. Batuecan	f. right whale
7. Azorean	g. antelope
8. Madeira	h. shrew
9. European	i. beetle
10. Aegean	j. bat
11. Saiga	k. brook newt
12. Bavarian	l. chamois
13. North Atlantic	m. mink
14. Montseny	n. lynx
15. Roach's	o. frog

EUROPE

64. MAKING MUSIC

The names of 15 instruments of the orchestra have been broken up in three letter-groups. Match a letter group in Column A with letters in Columns B and C to complete the name of an instrument.

	A	B	C	Instrument
1.	CL	OL	NI	________
2.	TR	UM	A	________
3.	BA	ANG	ONE	________
4.	TIM	ARI	ONE	________
5.	VIB	SS	E	________
6.	CY	CO	LE	________
7.	TR	B	HONE	________
8.	SAX	LU	ALS	________
9.	VI	PA	NET	________
10.	PIC	OMB	IN	________
11.	TU	BO	PET	________
12.	TRI	A	OON	________
13.	PI	RAP	TE	________
14.	O	OPH	LO	________
15.	F	MB	NO	________

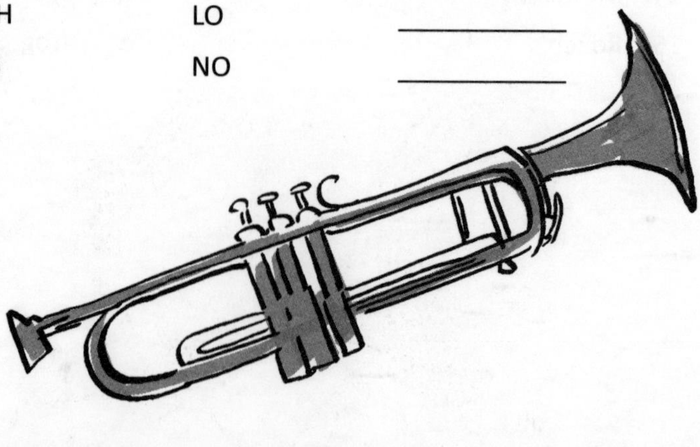

65. LINGUISTIC FERVOUR

Against each European language is a list of common English words, which have origin in that particular language. Pick the odd one out.

1. CZECH – pistol, candy, polka, robot
2. SWEDISH – tungsten, moped, ombudsman, macramé
3. DUTCH – beryl, bamboo, beleaguer, blaze
4. ITALIAN – antics, patina, sorbet, torso
5. FRENCH – magpie, grapefruit, cheroot, petticoat
6. HUNGARIAN – coach, ketchup, paprika, biro
7. IRISH – person, galore, slogan, banshee
8. PORTUGUESE – caste, lingo, marmalade, junk
9. RUSSIAN – glitch, balalaika, mammoth, sable
10. SCOTS – golf, raid, gingham, wraith

66. DAHL'S CHICKENS

Choose one letter from the letters given in the box and fill into the blanks to form the names of books written by famous children's author Roald Dahl.

A	B	C	D	E	F	G	H	I	J	L	M
N	O	P	R	S	T	U	V	W	X	Y	

1. THE MAGIC _ INGER
2. FA _ TASTIC MR. FO _
3. _ AMES AND THE GIANT _ EACH
4. CHA _ LIE AND THE CHOCOLATE FACTORY
5. M _ TIL _ A
6. THE _ FG
7. THE T _ ITS
8. THE WI _ CHES
9. GEORGE'S MAR _ ELLO _ S _ EDICINE
10. DANN _, THE C _ AMPION OF THE WORLD
11. BOY: TALES OF _ HILDHOOD
12. THE GR _ M _ INS
13. DIRTY BEA _ TS
14. _ OING SOL _
15. ES _ O TROT

67. FITTING THE ROLE

Match the names of the European film personalities with the films in which they had a leading role.

	Actor		Film
1.	Anthony Hopkins	a.	*The Best Exotic Marigold Hotel*
2.	Emma Watson	b.	*Inception*
3.	Colin Firth	c.	*Coco Before Chanel*
4.	Rachel Weisz	d.	*Peter Pan*
5.	Ludivine Sagnier	e.	*Noah*
6.	Judi Dench	f.	*Chocolat*
7.	Audrey Hepburn	g.	*Hannibal*
8.	Juliette Binoche	h.	*The Girl with the Dragon Tattoo*
9.	Gérard Depardieu	i.	*Bridget Jones' Diary*
10.	Audrey Tautou	j.	*Oz the Great and Powerful*
11.	Liam Neeson	k.	*The Lady in the Van*
12.	Ingrid Bergman	l.	*Taken*
13.	Maggie Smith	m.	*My Fair Lady*
14.	Marion Cotillard	n.	*The Man in the Iron Mask*
15.	Daniel Craig	o.	*Casablanca*

68. CROSSING TOWNS

Given below are the names of some towns in a European country. Use the lengths of the names to fill in the grid. Then, rearrange, the first letters of each town's name to find the name of the country to which these towns belong.

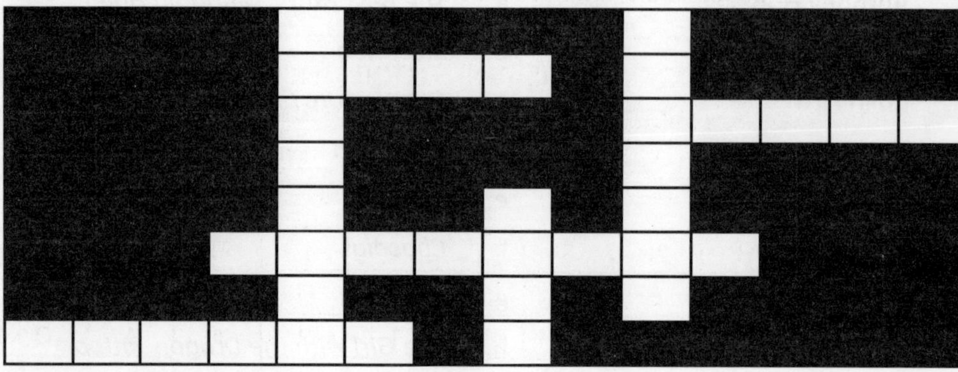

These towns belong to the country _ _ _ _ _ _ _ .

Arad (4)

Adjud (5)

Iași (4)

Mangalia (8)

Năvodari (8)

Orăștie (7)

Reghin (7)

EUROPE

69. LOOKING FOR A COUNTRY

Cross off the names of the towns and cities given below in the grid vertically and horizontally. Read the uncrossed letters across each row, and then across the next row and so on to find the name of the country in which these cities are located. A letter may be used more than once.

LOHNSFELD, LOOFT, LENSAHN, LOOP, LICHTE, LOSSATAL, LANGENTHAL, LINDEWITT, LYCHEN, LUXEM, LAUTRACH, LINDOW, LAWITZ, LAUGNA, LANZ, LAM, LIRSTAL, LECK, LEESE, LABENZ

L	O	H	N	S	F	E	L	D	N	P
I	K	G	E	M	E	X	U	L	H	O
C	C	E	S	E	E	L	R	A	A	O
H	E	L	A	B	E	N	Z	N	S	L
T	L	I	R	S	T	A	L	G	N	O
E	A	N	G	U	A	L	A	E	E	S
Z	T	I	W	A	L	Y	M	N	L	S
L	A	U	T	R	A	C	H	T	O	A
L	I	N	D	O	W	H	M	H	O	T
A	L	A	N	Z	N	E	Y	A	F	A
T	T	I	W	E	D	N	I	L	T	L

EUROPE

70. TRIBAL ROOTS

The names of some European gypsy tribes have been listed below. Place each name in the middle of a 'word box' so that you have three-letter words when you read the letters top down. You can only use four of the tribe names.

CASSI	NAUNES	ARVERNI	HERCATES
LUGII	SALYES	LICATES	LAPICINI

A P A A H

_ _ _ _ _

E N H P D

O F B A T U

_ _ _ _ _ _

E R D T E E

M I E R A I T

_ _ _ _ _ _ _

T E E D C K N

A D A T I D E F

_ _ _ _ _ _ _ _

L D T E E D D T

71. VISITING THE RIVIERA

Join two letter groups from the box below to get the names of famous European rivers. You have a clue for each: the name of a city through which the river flows.

DAN	TULA	RE	SE	GA	ELLE
BE	MOS	OD	PER	AL	LOI
TAG	ME	UBE	THA	RHO	RHI
MES	US	NE	INE	VIS	DNEI
ER	USE	NE	UR	VOL	EL

	City	River
1.	Warsaw	____________
2.	Toledo	____________
3.	Nantes	____________
4.	Maastricht	____________
5.	Frankfurt	____________
6.	Kiev	____________
7.	Vienna	____________
8.	Orenburg	____________

9. Nizhny Novgorod ____________________

10. Cologne ____________________

11. Dresden ____________________

12. Geneva ____________________

13. Paris ____________________

14. Trier ____________________

15. Reading ____________________

72. REMEMBERING RHYMES

How well do you remember the nursery rhymes you knew as a child? Do you know that almost all of these originated in Britain? Choose the correct answer from the options given below.

1. *Humpty Dumpty sat on a*: wall, stool, chair, horse
2. *Baa, baa, black sheep has three bags of*: hay, grass, wool, oats
3. *The little star twinkles in the sky like a*: crystal, diamond, beacon, torch
4. *Jack and Jill went up the*: ladder, wall, gate, hill
5. *Simple Simon met a*: cobbler, miller, pieman, journeyman
6. *Ring a ring of*: tulips, lilies, roses, dahlias
7. *Here we go round the*: mulberry bush, cactus shrub, money plant, herb garden
8. *Hickory, dickory, dock.____ ran up the clock?:* rat, mouse, squirrel, spider
9. *Little Miss Muffet sat on a*: table, rug, carpet, tuffet
10. *The three blind mice ran after the*: milkman's daughter, vegetable seller's son, farmer's wife, plumber's mother
11. *Mary had a little*: goat, lamb, calf, foal
12. *Little Bo Peep has lost her*: sheep, ribbon, shoe, plate

EUROPE

73. MISSING SCIENTISTS

Given below are clues to the names of some European scientists. Can you identify them? Fill one letter in each blank.

1. He developed the General Theory of Relativity – ______ ________
2. He arrived at a theory of evolution through natural selection – _______ ______
3. He discovered that when an object floats in a fluid it displaces a weight of the fluid equal to its own weight – __________
4. He formulated a model that said the sun was the centre of the universe, not the earth – __________
5. He formulated the laws of motion and gravity – _____ ______
6. She conducted pioneering research on radioactivity – _____ _____
7. His renown as a painter and technological genius made him the essential "Renaissance Man" – ________ __ _____
8. He has been called the father of observational astronomy and the father of modern physics – _______
9. He is renowned for his views of physical science, classical mechanics, logic and ethics – _________
10. He established the germ theory of disease and invented a process to stop foodstuffs going bad – _____ _______

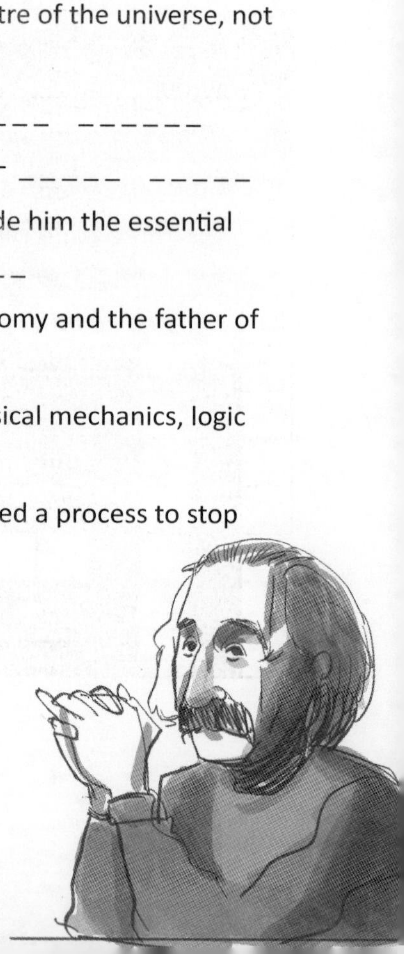

EUROPE

74. POLL-IT-I(C)S

Given below are the names of some prominent European political leaders. Use these to fill in the grid.

ANGELA MERKEL (GERMANY), BENITO MUSSOLINI (ITALY)
BERTIE AHERN (IRELAND), DOUGLAS HYDE (IRELAND)
EMIL BOC (ROMANIA), HELMUT KOHL (GERMANY)
ISA MUSTAFA (KOSOVO), JOSIP BROZ TITO (ERSTWHILE YUGOSLAVIA)
SALI BERISHA (ALBANIA), VLADIMIR LENIN (RUSSIA)

75. LET THERE BE PEACE!

Each set of letters has the name of a Nobel Peace Prize laureate and the country to which she/he belongs. Can you identify the country and the laureate? The first letter in each clue is also the first letter of the country's name.

1. P L E O C H L W A L A E N S D A
2. F M A I R N T T L I A A H T I S N A A D R I
3. I J R O E L H N H A N U D M E
4. U B N E I T T T Y E W D I K L I L N I G A D O M M S
5. F R R E N E C A A S S N I C N E
6. B D O E M I N I L Q G U E P I U I M R E
7. S A L W V A E M Y D R E D N A L

76. PITA IN THE CAPITAL

Each three-letter group given below is contained in the name of a North American country's capital city. Can you identify these capitals?

3-letter group	**Capital**
EXAMPLE: NGT	**WASHINGTON DC**
1. GEO	______________
2. TAU	______________
3. TOF	______________
4. TON	______________
5. NAG	______________
6. GET	______________
7. VAN	______________
8. ASS	______________
9. MAC	______________
10. JOS	______________

NORTH AMERICA

77. COLD WORDS

Cross out the words given below vertically, horizontally and diagonally. Read the uncrossed letters across each row to find what these words have in common.

BLUWID	CHAHATLIN	CHIUP	CLIM	EROLINYAT
KATIYANA	KRIKAYA	MENTLANA	NAKLIN	NYIK
QINYAYA	TALINI	TLAMO	TLALMAN	TLUN

K	A	T	I	Y	A	N	A	T
N	A	P	S	N	O	K	B	A
I	I	Y	U	M	R	I	L	Y
L	C	L	A	I	N	Y	U	N
T	T	L	K	Y	H	N	W	I
A	T	A	I	A	N	C	I	L
H	Y	O	W	M	N	I	D	O
A	T	A	L	I	N	I	Q	R
H	T	L	A	L	M	A	N	E
C	A	N	A	L	T	N	E	M

78. STATING THE OBVIOUS

The names of two states of the United States of America are squished together on each line below. All the letters are in the correct order, separate the two names. The first two letters are the first letters in the names of each of the states.

1. I C L O L L I O N R O A I D S O
2. U I T O W A H A
3. M V I A R R G I Y L N A I N A D
4. O K R E A N G S A O S N
5. M W I I S S S C O O N U S R I I N
6. P C E O N N N N S E Y C L T V I A C N U I A T
7. L T O E U I N N E S I A S S N E A
8. A N R I E Z V O A N D A A
9. A M L O A N S T A K N A A
10. N A E R B K A R N A S S A S K A

79. STATES OF MYSTERY

Arrange the names of the states listed below into the grid. Once you are done, read the shaded column top down to find the name of the country in which they are located.

COLIMA, HIDALGO, MORELOS, OAXACA, SONORA, TLAXCALA

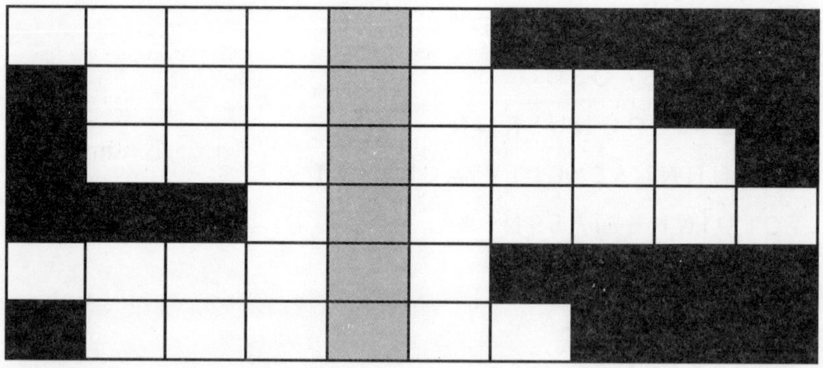

80. MONEY MATCH

Match the name of the North American country in Column A with its currency in Column B, and the fractional unit of its currency in Column C.

Country		Currency		Fractional Unit	
1.	Haiti	a.	Córdoba	i.	Centavo
2.	Panama	b.	Peso	ii.	Centavo
3.	Guatemala	c.	Colón	iii.	Centavo
4.	Nicaragua	d.	Lempira	iv.	Centavo
5.	Dominican Republic	e.	Balboa	v.	Centésimo
6.	Costa Rica	f.	Gourde	vi.	Centime
7.	Honduras	g.	Quetzal	vii.	Céntimo

NORTH AMERICA

81. CARTOON CHARACTERS

Match the names of the North American TV programs in the first column with the names of their main characters in the second column.

TV Programme		Character	
1.	*The Batman*	a.	Uncle Rico
2.	*The Marvellous Misadventures of Flapjack*	b.	Nigel Uno
3.	*Clifford the Big Red Dog*	c.	Miranda Isabella Sanchez
4.	*The Fairly OddParents*	d.	Shego
5.	*Dora the Explorer*	e.	Tino Tonitini
6.	*Lizzie McGuire*	f.	Boots
7.	*The Weekenders*	g.	Captain K'nuckles
8.	*Kim Possible*	h.	Timmy Turner
9.	*Codename: Kids Next Door*	i.	Emily Elizabeth
10.	*Corneil and Bernie*	j.	Bruce Wayne

82. EMBLEMATIC PRIDE

Use the clues to identify the North American country which is described.

1. This flag features isosceles triangles evoking the lava rocks found in the country. ____________________
2. This flag features the country's national emblem of an eagle clutching a snake in its talons and beak. ____________________
3. This flag features the country's national coat of arms showing two workers standing in the shade of a mahogany tree. ____________________
4. This flag has three green diamonds in the middle with a yellow stripe. ____________________
5. This flag features the rising sun. ____________________
6. This flag features a coat of arms that depicts a shield supported by a palm and an olive branch. ____________________
7. This flag features a maple leaf. ____________________
8. This flag has a diagonal black stripe. ____________________
9. This flag depicts the national bird of the country holding a scroll. ____________________
10. This flag features a black trident. ____________________
11. This flag has two diagonal yellow stripes. ____________________
12. This flag features a black triangle and a yellow stripe. ____________________

83. ROUTE IT THIS WAY

Choose one letter from the letters in the box below and fill it into a blank such that the word forms the name of a junction on US Route 20, which runs across the United States from west to east. Each letter is used only once.

B	C	D	F	G	H	K	L	M
N	P	R	S	T	V	W	X	Y

1. _ EW _ ORT, Oregon
2. AL _ AN _, Oregon
3. CAL _ _ ELL, Idaho
4. SIOU _ CI _ Y, Indiana
5. ROC _ FO _ D, Illinois
6. C _ ICA _ O, Illinois
7. _ LE _ ELAND, Ohio
8. BUFFA _ O, New York
9. _ PRING _ IELD, Massachusetts
10. WALTHA _, Massachusetts

84. ADDING UP TO IT

Join two letter groups from the box below to find out the capital cities of these North American countries.

John's	ries	basse	ott
galpa	santo	eau	teguci
cast	belm	awa	terre
domingo	saint	ros	opan

1. Saint Lucia ______________________
2. Honduras ______________________
3. Dominica ______________________
4. Antigua and Barbuda ______________________
5. Saint Kitts and Nevis ______________________
6. Canada ______________________
7. Belize ______________________
8. Dominican Republic ______________________

85. MAKE A MATCH

Match the names of the provinces in the first column with their capitals in the second column. Do you know which country they belong to?

Province		Capital	
1.	New Brunswick	a.	Regina
2.	Alberta	b.	Halifax
3.	Saskatchewan	c.	Victoria
4.	Prince Edward Island	d.	Edmonton
5.	Nova Scotia	e.	Winnipeg
6.	British Columbia	f.	Charlottetown
7.	Manitoba	g.	Fredericton

86. ISLAND FUN

The names of seven major islands have been broken up into three-letter groups. Match a letter group in Column A with letters in Columns B and C to complete the name of an island. There is also an eighth island, which has the same name as the group of these eight islands. Can you guess the name of the eighth island and what the group of islands is called?

	A	B	C	Island
1.	Ma	a	we	___________
2.	Ni	ua	i	___________
3.	Ka	ola	hu	___________
4.	O	ok	au	___________
5.	La	u	i	___________
6.	Mol	na	ai	___________
7.	Kaho	ih	i	___________

87. ENDANGERED AND MISSING

Choose one letter from the letters given below and fill it into a blank such that the word forms the name of an endangered animal in North America. Each letter is used only once.

A	B	C	D	E	F	G	H	I	J	K	L	M
N	O	P	Q	R	S	T	U	V	W	X	Y	Z

1. _ EMPOALTEPEC VO _ E – Mexico
2. BROWN'S HU _ _ A – Jamaica
3. _ A _ UITA – Mexico
4. HAWAIIAN HOAR _ _ AT – Hawaii
5. ROATAN ISLAND A _ O _ TI – Honduras
6. HAITIAN _ OL _ NODON – Dominican Republic
7. _ A G U A R U N _ I – Costa Rica, Mexico, Nicaragua, Panama, USA
8. SAN JOAQUIN KIT _ O _ – USA
9. WOODLAND _ ARIB _ U – Canada, USA
10. YUCATAN BRO _ N BROC _ ET DEER – Belize, Guatemala, Mexico
11. VANCOUVER ISLAND M _ _ MOT – Canada
12. _ RONG _ ORN – USA
13. BULLER'S CHIP _ U _ K – Mexico

88. POINTING UP

Solve the clues given in the brackets to find the correct words. Then, use the number of letters mentioned next to it to fill the blanks. You will get the names of the highest mountain peaks of these North American countries.

FOR EXAMPLE: _ _ _ A LISA (THE FIRST WORKING DAY OF THE WEEK - 3)

The first working day of the week is MONDAY. By putting the first 3 letters of MONDAY in the blanks, we get MONA LISA, the name of a famous painting.

1. _ _ _ O DU _ _ _ E – Dominican Republic

   (Short form of another word for image – 3, paintings, drawings etc. - 3)

2. PIC LA _ _ _ _ E – Haiti (The opposite of 'buy' – 4)

3. _ _ _ _ _ _ _ _ _ _ _ _ PEAK – Jamaica (A primary colour – 4, a tall hill - 8)

4. PICO _ _ _ _ _ INO – Cuba

   (A light blue colour, also a semi-precious stone - 5)

5. _ _ _ _ E DIA _ _ _ _ INS – Dominica

   (The time before 12 noon – 4, to soak up or remove excess ink with paper – 4)

6. LA _ _ _ _ RIERE – Saint Vincent and the Grenadines

   (A baked dish made of egg yolks and beaten egg whites - 4)

7. MOUNT _ _ _ _ UIGA – Saint Kitts and Nevis

   (The first name of famous Hollywood actor Neeson – 4)

8. _ _ _ _ _ _ – Alaska, USA

   (where the lion lives – 3, a famous first name in Arabian folk tales – 3)

9. MOUNT _ _ _ AN – Canada

   (A part of the trunk or large branch of a tree – 3)

10. _ _ _ O _ _ _ E _ _ _ L – Mexico

    (The husband of 'Mom' – 3, mice run from it – 3, an animal you keep in your house – 3)

89. NAME THE PARK

Take a group of letters from the box below and place it in the blank spaces on each line to end the name of a person and begin the name of a national park or reserve. Cross off each group of letters as you use it.

SH	IN	IS	CH
NE	AR	LE	EL
ME	CA	JA	SE

1. EL/__/VERA (Grenada)
2. CATHERI/__/GRIL (Jamaica)
3. LOU/__/LA CABRITOS (Dominican Republic)
4. REBEC/__/GUANES (Cuba)
5. TRI/__/ENANDOAH (United States)
6. OSC/__/RECIFE ALACRANES (Mexico)
7. JERO/__/LAJO (Trinidad and Tobago)
8. MIT/__/AGRE (Panama)
9. COL/__/AGUA (Bahamas)
10. KHADI/__/SPER (Canada)
11. LOUI/__/LVA NEGRA (Nicaragua)
12. LION/__/ ROSARIO (Guatemala)

90. JUMBLED HEADS

Unscramble the letters below to find the names of 10 famous presidents of the United States.

1.	REGGOE	INTHAWSONG	– _ _ _ _ _ _ _ _ _ _ _ _ _ _ _ _
2.	MATHSO	FORNEFSEJ	– _ _ _ _ _ _ _ _ _ _ _ _ _ _ _
3.	HARMBAA	CILLONN	– _ _ _ _ _ _ _ _ _ _ _ _ _ _
4.	ROODWOW	SWOLIN	– _ _ _ _ _ _ _ _ _ _ _ _ _
5.	HONJ	YENDENK	– _ _ _ _ _ _ _ _ _ _ _
6.	HIDTGW	NOWISHEREE	– _ _ _ _ _ _ _ _ _ _ _ _ _ _ _ _
7.	IMAWLIL	NICTOLN	– _ _ _ _ _ _ _ _ _ _ _ _ _ _
8.	FINKNARL	LOREVOSET	– _ _ _ _ _ _ _ _ _ _ _ _ _ _ _ _ _
9.	OJNH	MASAD	– _ _ _ _ _ _ _ _ _
10.	RAYHR	MUTNAR	– _ _ _ _ _ _ _ _ _ _ _

NORTH AMERICA

91. NOBLE IS AS NOBEL DOES

Given below are the names of some Nobel Prize laureates from North America. Match the names to the country from which each person hails, and the field in which s/he received the prize.

	Nobel Prize laureate	Country	Field
1.	VS Naipaul, 2001	a. Saint Lucia	i. Economics
2.	Alfonso Garcia Robles, 1982	b. Guatemala	ii. Literature
3.	Sir Arthur Lewis, 1979	c. Canada	iii. Peace
4.	David J Wineland, 2012	d. Mexico	iv. Physics
5.	Ralph M Steinman, 2011 Medicine	e. Guatemala	v. Physiology or
6.	Óscar Arias Sanchez, 1987	f. United States	vi. Political Activism
7.	Miguel Ángel Asturias, 1967	g. United States	vii. Chemistry
8.	Mario Jose Molina Henriquez, 1995	h. Trinidad and Tobago	viii. Peace
9.	Rigoberta Menchú, 1992	i. Canada	ix. Literature
10.	Derek Walcott, 1992	j. Canada	x. Economics
11.	Willard S Boyle, 2009	k. Costa Rica	xi. Literature
12.	Thomas Schelling, 2005	l. Mexico	xii. Astrophysics
13.	Carol W Greider, 200	m. United States	xiii. Biochemistry
14.	Arthur B McDonald, 2015 or Medicine	n. United States	xiv. Molecular Biology
15.	Robert J Lefkowitz, 2012	o. Saint Lucia	xv. Physics

92. CLASSIC AMERICANA

Against each classic American novel is a scrambled word. Unscramble it to find the name of its author.

1. *The Grapes of Wrath* – OJNH BINCTSKEE _ _ _ _ _ _ _ _ _ _ _ _ _ _
2. *The Color Purple* – CELIA WRAKEL _ _ _ _ _ _ _ _ _ _ _
3. *On the Road* – KACJ CUREOAK _ _ _ _ _ _ _ _ _ _ _
4. *To Kill a Mockingbird* – PHREAR ELE _ _ _ _ _ _ _ _ _
5. *Slaughterhouse Five* – RUKT GENTUNOV _ _ _ _ _ _ _ _ _ _ _ _
6. *The Portrait of a Lady* – NYHER MASJE _ _ _ _ _ _ _ _ _ _
7. *Adventures of Huckleberry Finn* – AKRM WANTI _ _ _ _ _ _ _ _ _
8. *Atlas Shrugged* – YAN DARN _ _ _ _ _ _ _
9. *Fahrenheit 451* – AYR DRABYRUB _ _ _ _ _ _ _ _ _ _ _
10. *The Crucible* – TRURAH LEMRIL _ _ _ _ _ _ _ _ _ _ _ _
11. *Beloved* – ONTI RIMORONS _ _ _ _ _ _ _ _ _ _ _ _
12. *I Know Why the Caged Bird Sings* – AYMA ULOANGE

    _ _ _ _ _ _ _ _ _ _ _
13. *Uncle Tom's Cabin* – ARTHEIR HEREBEC WETSO

    _ _ _ _ _ _ _ _ _ _ _ _ _ _ _ _ _ _ _
14. *For Whom the Bell Tolls* – RENETS WHIMYNAGE

    _ _ _ _ _ _ _ _ _ _ _ _ _ _ _ _
15. *The Scarlet Letter* – LATEINNHA WENTHORAH

    _ _ _ _ _ _ _ _ _ _ _ _ _ _ _ _ _ _

93. SHE'S SIMPLY THE BEST!

Given below are the names of movies in which the female lead won the Academy Award for Best Actress in a Leading Role. Insert the name of the actress into each row. When you are done, read down the shaded column to find the name of an actress who has won the maximum number of Academy Awards for Best Actress in a Leading Role.

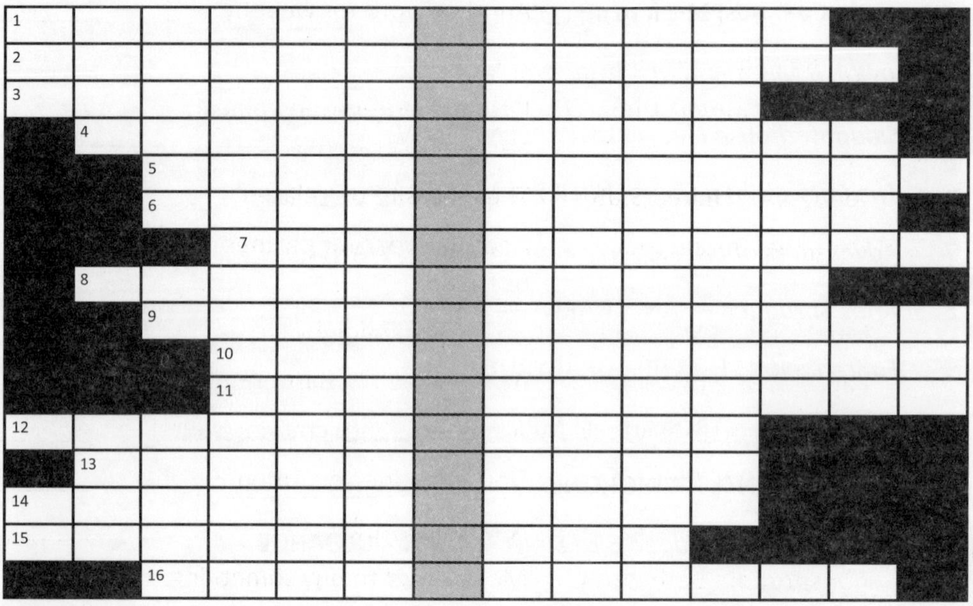

Clues:

1. *The Hours*
2. *Dead Man Walking*
3. *The Iron Lady*
4. *Howards End*
5. *Erin Brockovich*
6. *Million Dollar Baby*
7. *The Silence of the Lambs*
8. *Gone With the Wind*
9. *Mary Poppins*
10. *Two Women*
11. *The Reader*
12. *Coal Miner's Daughter*
13. *Monster's Ball*
14. *The Piano*
15. *Room*
16. *The Queen*

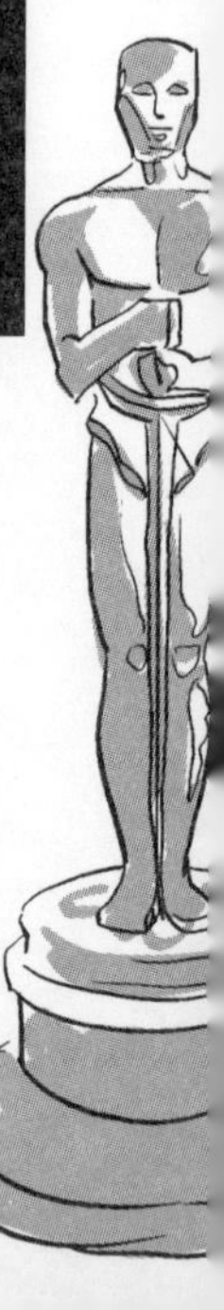

94. WHAT'S IN THE RIVER?

The name of each North American river below contains a word that fits the clue given in the second column. Find this word

River	Clue	Answer
EXAMPLE: ~~G~~ A ~~N~~ G E ~~S~~, India	**The noun for how old a person is**	**AGE**
1. Rio Conchos, Mexico	Another word for wealthy	________
2. Machaquila, Guatemala	The postman delivers this	________
3. Sagua La Grande, Cuba	Pituitary, adrenal and pineal are examples of this	________
4. Tennessee, United States	The opposite of 'relaxed'	________
5. Manatee, Belize	Another word for partner or friend	________
6. Montrouis, Haiti	The sound made by a cow	________
7. Papaloteca, Honduras	A secret plan to harm someone	________
8. Sensunapan, El Salvador	A sudden, sharp cracking sound	________
9. Martha Brae, Jamaica	Not occurring very often	________
10. Calovebora, Panama	A warming spice	________
11. Constitution, Barbados	Money paid to buy something	________
12. Crayfish, Dominica	A violent collision	________

95. DOT WHAT?

Match the names of North American countries with their country code top-level domains (TLD). For instance, Indian sites would have .in to show it is an Indian website.

	Country		Country Code TLD
1.	Panama	a.	.lc
2.	Belize	b.	.jm
3.	Dominica	c.	.cu
4.	Grenada	d.	.pa
5.	Honduras	e.	.do
6.	Saint Vincent and the Grenadines	f.	.tt
7.	Cuba	g.	.kn
8.	Haiti	h.	.bb
9.	Nicaragua	i.	.cr
10.	Bahamas	j.	.ni
11.	Antigua and Barbuda	k.	.dm
12.	Costa Rica	l.	.sv
13.	Saint Lucia	m.	.hn
14.	Jamaica	n.	.bz
15.	Barbados	o.	.gt
16.	Trinidad and Tobago	p.	.gd
17.	El Salvador	q.	.ht
18.	Guatemala	r.	.vc
19.	Dominican Republic	s.	.bs
20.	Saint Kitts and Nevis	t.	.ag

ORTH AMERICA

96. TRIBAL WISDOM

Solve the clues, putting one letter on each blank. Then insert the letters according to the numbers given below into the sentences. Some of the blanks do not have number clues below them, and are marked 'X'. See if you can fill in these blanks too to find proverbs of three Native American tribes.

What Sumo fighters do : _ _ _ _ _ _ _
1 2 3 4 5 6 3

Adam and Eve ate from the Tree of? : _ _ _ _ _ _ _ _ _
7 8 9 1 6 3 10 11 3

The unit of parents with children : _ _ _ _ _ _
12 13 14 15 6 16

A boxer's blow or a fruit drink : _ _ _ _ _
17 18 8 19 20

1. "_ _   _ _   _ _ _ _ _ _   _ _ _ _ _ _,   _ _ _   _ _ _ _
15 12   1 3   1 9 8 10 3 2   9 12 5 3 8   5 20 3   11 15 12 5

_ _   _ _ _ _ _ _ _ _ _   _ _ _ _   _ _ _ _."
9 12   7 8 9 1 6 3 10 11 3   1 15 6 6   19 9 14 3

~ _ _ _ _ _ _ _
13 2 13 17 13 20 9

2. “_ _ _   _ _ _ _ _ _   _ _ _ _ _ _   _ _ _ _   _   _ _ _ _ _ _.”

9 8 3   12 1 8 11 3 2   19 13 8 8 9 5   6 15 12 5   13   17 3 X X 6 3

~ _ _ _ _

20 9 17 15

3. “_ _ _’ _   _ _ _   _ _ _ _ _ _ _ _ _   _ _ _   _ _

10 9 8 5   6 3 5   16 3 4 5 3 2 10 13 16   18 4 3   18 17

_ _ _   _ _ _ _   _ _   _ _ _ _ _.”

5 9 9   14 18 19 20   9 12   5 9 10 13 16

~ _ _ _ _ _ _ _ _

19 20 3 2 9 7 3 3

97. WHO RUN THE WORLD? GIRLS!

Match the names of the North American women singers in the first column with their hit singles in the second column.

Singer	**Hit Single**
1. Céline Dion	a. *All I Ask of You*
2. Adele	b. *We Belong Together*
3. Beyoncé	c. *Forever and For Always*
4. Whitney Houston	d. *Don't Know Much*
5. Madonna	e. *Single Ladies*
6. Mariah Carey	f. *How Was I to Know*
7. Shania Twain	g. *My Heart Will Go On*
8. Reba McEntire	h. *I Wanna Dance With Somebody*
9. Barbra Streisand	i. *Hello*
10. Linda Ronstadt	j. *Papa Don't Preach*

98. TESTING TIMES

Hidden in the grid below is a famous quote by Abraham Lincoln, the 16th President of the United States. Read across each row from left to right, crossing out unnecessary letters to find it.

N	E	A	R	L	Y	P	O	A	L	L	C
X	M	E	N	D	U	N	C	A	N	C	O
O	L	I	N	S	T	A	N	D	R	I	M
D	A	A	D	V	E	R	S	I	T	Y	B
B	U	T	A	I	F	F	O	T	Y	O	U
R	W	A	N	T	B	I	T	O	B	Y	E
T	E	S	T	L	A	S	A	M	A	N	S
C	H	A	R	A	C	T	E	R	P	E	R
G	I	V	E	S	U	M	H	I	M	E	T
I	S	S	T	O	P	O	W	E	R	L	A

99. MUSICAL MATCH

Match the names of the North American musicians in the first column with the country in which they were born in the second column.

Singer	**Country of Birth**
1. Ricky Martin	a. Barbados
2. Gloria Estefan	b. Jamaica
3. Carlos Santana	c. Puerto Rico (territory of the US)
4. Rihanna	d. Mexico
5. Wyclef Jean	e. Cuba
6. Bob Marley	f. El Salvador
7. Billy Ocean	g. Mexico
8. Thalia	h. Dominican Republic
9. Juan Luis Guerra	i. Haiti
10. Álvaro Torres	j. Trinidad and Tobago

100. GOLDEN WORDS

Unscramble each word to find a quote by Martin Luther King Jr, an American Baptist minister and prominent leader of the African-American Civil Rights movement.

"EHT ETMI SI SWAYLA GRITH OT OD

"___ ____ __ ______ _____ __ __

HATW SI ITRGH."

____ __ _____."

101. MASKED COUNTRY

Find the South American countries hidden in the following sentences.

1. The portable hibachi lets you cook wherever you are.
2. Have you ever seen a guy analyse other guys?
3. The antelope rubbed itself against the tree.
4. This tiramisu, Rina, melts in the mouth.
5. Grab Olivia before she overturns the boiling kettle!
6. I've studied algebra zillions of times, but still can't understand it.
7. Vulgar gent in a vulgar suit—that's how I'd describe him.
8. The Col Om biannual trophy is awarded for excellence in leadership.

102. CITIES MAKE A COUNTRY

Arrange the names of the states listed below into the grid. Once you are done, read the shaded column top down to find the name of the country in which they are located.

CURITIBA FORTALEZA LONDRINA MANAUS NATAL RECIFEA

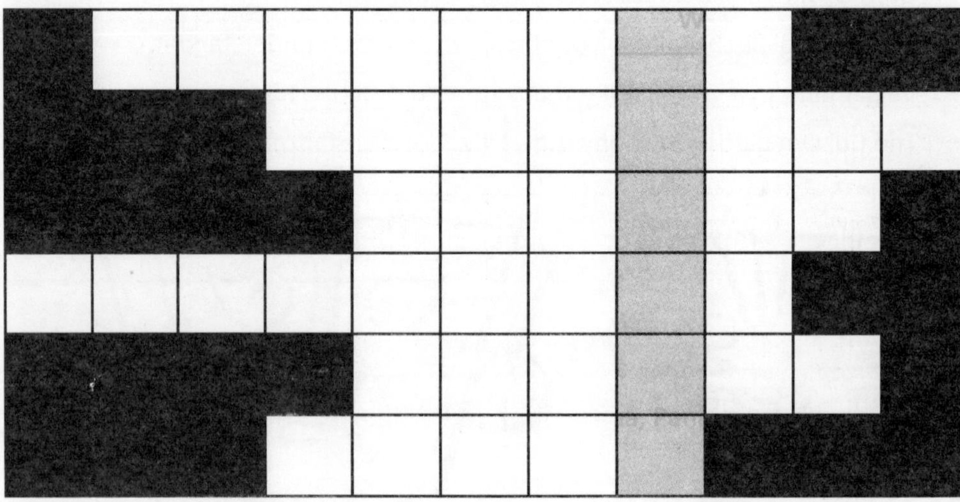

103. CAPITAL CHAOS

Hidden in the grid are 10 capitals of South American countries. The countries have been given as clues. Locate all the capitals horizontally, vertically and diagonally.

N	R	S	V	A	N	P	C	L	O
O	W	M	A	N	T	A	Q	E	Z
I	M	O	J	N	Y	O	D	R	S
C	Y	Z	T	E	T	I	G	A	D
N	R	E	N	E	V	I	C	O	J
U	L	N	L	E	G	A	A	Q	B
S	E	I	T	N	R	R	U	G	D
A	L	N	M	A	A	I	O	B	O
K	O	R	C	A	T	T	R	E	D
M	R	K	L	O	L	T	S	T	G

1. Venezuela
2. Ecuador
3. Guyana
4. Paraguay
5. Chile
6. Falkland Islands
7. Peru
8. Colombia
9. French Guiana
10. Uruguay

104. FOUND ONLY HERE

Choose one letter from the letters in the box below and fill in the blank such that the word forms the name of an animal or bird naturally found only in South America. Each letter is used only once.

A	B	C	E	F	G	H	H	I	L
M	N	O	P	R	S	T	U	W	Y

1. GIAN _ TORTOI _ E
2. ANACO _ DA
3. SOUTHERN RIGHT _ HALE
4. CAP _ _ ARA
5. AND _ AN CONDO _
6. MARINE IG _ ANA
7. FLIGHTLESS _ OR _ ORANT
8. GALAPAGOS _ INC _ ES
9. GALAPAGOS _ EN _ UINS
10. MAGNIFICENT FR _ G _ TEBIRD
11. LARGE PAINTED _ _ CUSTS
12. GOL_EN LION TAMA _ I _

105. JUMBLED, PRIZED BOOKS

Against each book's name is a scrambled word. Unscramble each to find the name of a Nobel Prize winner for literature. The country to which he/she belong has been given as a clue.

1. *All the Odes* – BOPAL RADENU (Chile) _ _ _ _ _ _ _ _ _ _ _ _ _ _
2. *Desolation* – LABARGEI RAMTSLI (Chile) _ _ _ _ _ _ _ _ _ _ _ _ _ _ _
3. *The Feast of the Goat* – ROIAM GRASVA SLALO (Peru) _ _ _ _ _ _ _ _ _ _ _ _ _ _ _ _
4. *Love in the Time of Cholera* – BILAGER CARAIG QARMUZE (Colombia) _

106. THE AWE-INSPIRING INCAS

Fill in the blanks to make the names of animals or birds. Then, read down the blanks to get the name of one emperor and one deity of the Incas.

_ LLIGATOR	_ ULTURE
_ URKEY	_ BIS
_ NT	_ AM
_ ORSE	_ LBATROSS
_ MBRELLABIRD	_ IVET
_ ARDVARK	_ WL
_ OBSTER	_ OUGAR
_ IGEON	_ YENA
_ RMADILLO	_ NTEATER

— — — — — — — — — (emperor)

— — — — — — — — — (deity)

107. TRIBAL GAPS

In each puzzle pair, the first three letters are the same. Solve the clues to find the three letters, and then put them in word given below to find the name of a South American tribe found in the country/countries given in brackets.

Y A N K E D (pulled hard)

Y A N O M A M I (indigenous people of Brazil and Venezuela)

_ _ _ U E (a line in which to wait)

_ _ _ C H U A (Colombia, Ecuador, Peru, Bolivia, Argentina and Chile)

_ _ _ N O (a large musical instrument)

_ _ _ R O A (Colombia and Venezuela)

_ _ _ M (the part of your hand that has lines)

_ _ _ I K U R (Brazil, French Guiana)

_ _ _ L E (you pull a chair up to it)

_ _ _ A H A R A (Brazil)

_ _ _ R I N A (Russian female ruler)

_ _ _ C H I L A (Ecuador)

_ _ _ Z I N G (astonishing)

_ _ _ I C H A (Argentina)

_ _ _ N G E (alter)

_ _ _ N G O (Chile)

_ _ _ B E R (this person may give you a shave)

_ _ _ A (Colombia)

_ _ _ K E R E L (a type of fish)

_ _ _ H I G U E N G A (Peru)

_ _ _ L A I N (the evil one opposing the hero)

_ _ _ E L A (Argentina)

_ _ _ D (a beach is made of this)

_ _ _ A P A N A (Paraguay)

_ _ _ G T H (multiplied by breadth, this gives area)

_ _ _ G U A (Paraguay)

108. LIFE-GIVING WATERS

Join together two separate word sections from the box below to make the six-letter word that answers each clue. Write the word in the grid going downward. Each three-letter piece is used only once, so you can cross it off. When the grid is completed, read across the shaded rows to find the names of two South American rivers.

ADY	ZEN	RNS	ADO	NOM	PTS
ADO	ADS	ORA	MAL	NGE	ANA

1	2	3	4	5	6

Clues:

1. Legally brings up another's child as one's own
2. Illness
3. Decorates
4. Part of the house reserved for women
5. A colour
6. Those who travel from place to place and have no permanent home

109. MOVE TO THE BEAT

Given in the box are the names of dances of a South American country. Arrange the names into the grid and read down the shaded column to find the name of the country to which these dances belong.

CARNAVALITO, CHAMAMÉ, CHACARERA, CUARTETO, CUECA
CUMBIA VILLERA, MURGA, TANGO, ZAMBA

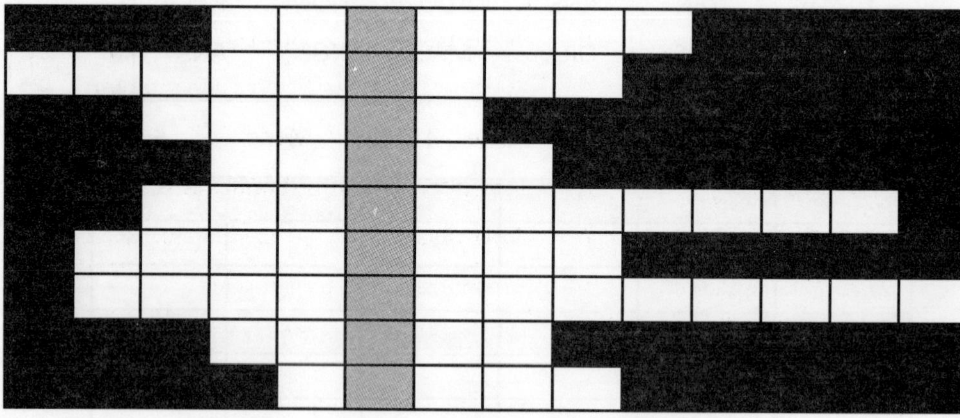

110. FAME IS WHAT FAME DOES

Match the names of famous South Americans, in (column one) with their native country (column two) and their professions (column three).

Famous Personality		Country		Profession	
1.	Juan Pablo Montoya	a.	Peru	(i)	Fashion designer
2.	ER Braithwaite	b.	Ecuador	(ii)	Guerilla leader
3.	Isabel Allende	c.	Paraguay	(iii)	Banker
4.	Carlos Noriega	d.	Venezuela	(iv)	Violinist, conductor
5.	Ernesto "Che" Guevara	e.	Brazil	(v)	Painter and sculptor
6.	Bárbara Mori	f.	Chile	(vi)	Model
7.	Jaime Laredo	g.	Argentina	(vii)	Professional footballer
8.	Carolina Herrera	h.	Colombia	(viii)	Teacher, diplomat
9.	Oswaldo Guayasamín	i.	Colombia	(ix)	Astronaut
10.	Augusto Roa Bastos	j.	Uruguay	(x)	Writer
11.	Gisele Bündchen	k.	Brazil	(xi)	Singer, songwriter
12.	Edgar Davids	l.	Argentina	(xii)	Race car driver
13.	Juan Martín del Potro	m.	Bolivia	(xiii)	Tennis player
14.	Joseph Safra	n.	Guyana	(xiv)	Actor
15.	Shakira	o.	Suriname	(xv)	Novelist, short story writer

111. RI-O-LYMPICS

In 2016, the Olympic Games were held for the first time in South America at Rio de Janeiro, Brazil. Test your knowledge of the Rio Olympics.

1. Three teams were first-time participants in the Olympics. Name them.
2. Olympic football matches were held in five cities in Brazil. One of them was Belo Horizante. Name the other four.
3. In which stadium did the opening and closing ceremonies take place?
4. Name the mascot of the Rio Olympic Games.
5. What does the slogan of the Games—*Viva sua paixao*—translate to in English?
6. Which two games were added back to the Olympics after more than 90 years?
7. The Olympic cauldron was to be lit by this famous Brazilian originally, but he declined due to health reasons. Name him.
8. The cauldron was lit by Vanderlei Cordeiro de Lima, men's marathon bronze medallist at the 2004 Olympics, who was awarded another medal for sportsmanship by the IOC after being attacked by a spectator and losing his lead. Name the other medal.
9. Which sportsperson won the maximum number of medals in the Rio Olympics, and for which sport?
10. Name the virus that raised significant health and safety concerns during the Games.

112. HOW RESOURCEFUL!

The names of various natural resources and the countries in which they are found have been mixed together. The first letter is the first letter of the country name, and the second letter is the first letter in the name of the natural resource. Letters have been placed in the correct order. Separate the letters and write the name of each country and its natural resource in the blanks.

1. C O L C O O M A B L I A

   Country: ________________ Natural resource: ________________

2. B I R R O N A O Z R I E L

   Country: ________________ Natural resource: ________________

3. C M O H L Y B I D E L N U E M

   Country: ________________ Natural resource: ________________

4. P C E O P R P U E R

   Country: ________________ Natural resource: ________________

5. B T O L I I V N I A

   Country: ________________ Natural resource: ________________

6. G B U A Y U X A I N T A E

   Country: ________________ Natural resource: ________________

7. A L R I M G E E S N T T I O N N A E

Country: ________________ Natural resource: ________________

8. U M R A U R G B U A L Y E

Country: ________________ Natural resource: ________________

9. B M O A N L G I A V N I A E S E

Country: ________________ Natural resource: ________________

10. P S I E L V R E U R

Country: ________________ Natural resource: ________________

113. COMPREENDO PORTUGUESE

Try your hand at understanding Portuguese. Choose the correct meaning of each Portuguese word from the options given.

1. Sim – some, slow, small, yes
2. Agua – fire, water, guard, out
3. Corpo – body, corporation, cooperate, company
4. Enfermeira – fern, entry, nurse, more
5. Relogio – logic, clock, relocate, loghouse
6. Fazer – faze, haze, phase, do
7. Longe – far, long, late, lozenge
8. Bom – boom, bomb, good, blimp
9. Bonito – bonobo, beautiful, boon, banter
10. Nunca – never, nurse, nun, nice
11. Tempo – speed, pace, rhythm, time
12. Dia – diameter, diagram, day, dial
13. Vida – life, video, vital, love
14. Desculpe – design, sculpture, statue, excuse me
15. Obrigado – brigadier, thank you, obliged, gardenia

114. PROTECTING THE ENDANGERED

Hidden in the grid are 14 near-threatened, vulnerable and critically endangered animals of the Amazonian rainforest. Look for them horizontally, vertically and diagonally.

B	G	O	L	D	E	N	L	I	O	N	T	A	M	A	R	I	N
G	R	H	Y	A	C	I	N	T	H	M	A	C	A	W	B	M	K
O	G	O	H	H	T	O	L	S	D	E	O	T	E	E	R	H	T
R	I	W	W	K	N	M	R	J	T	X	L	L	T	B	T	M	G
F	A	P	N	N	V	I	Q	E	Y	B	G	X	L	P	O	W	B
T	N	X	Y	T	S	M	H	P	T	A	M	U	K	U	J	Y	M
R	T	L	Q	G	G	P	Y	P	E	T	E	Q	N	Y	B	W	N
A	A	B	E	L	M	B	I	Y	L	P	O	T	W	X	T	W	M
D	R	Y	Z	A	L	Y	P	D	O	O	A	T	T	M	T	M	Y
N	M	K	R	Y	R	R	M	I	E	I	D	W	N	L	X	Q	M
O	A	V	M	A	A	S	S	A	N	R	X	K	P	A	Y	V	D
S	D	Z	B	H	U	O	M	T	R	T	M	Y	N	L	I	B	Y
I	I	Q	D	B	N	G	A	A	G	M	X	O	G	I	Q	G	R
O	L	B	R	F	M	P	A	K	C	K	O	R	N	J	P	P	L
P	L	L	R	Q	I	N	R	J	R	A	J	S	Y	K	V	D	N
Y	O	O	B	R	Q	T	J	Y	Z	R	W	Q	E	R	E	T	R
D	G	Q	Y	R	Z	T	Y	M	Z	R	M	N	J	T	G	Y	D

BLUE POISON FROG	BROWN SPIDER MONKEY	GIANT ARMADILLO
GIANT OTTER	GOLDEN LION TAMARIN	HARPY EAGLE
HYACINTH MACAW	JAGUAR	LEAR'S MACAW
MOUNTAIN TAPIR	PINK DOLPHIN	POISON DART FROG
PYGMY MARMOSET	THREE-TOED SLOTH	

115. UNLOCK THE FLAVOURS

Here are some national foods of South American countries. Use the code, in the box, to unlock the names of the dishes.

1. Brazil – A stew of beans with beef and port & * " ¶ < @ ^ @

   __ __ __ __ __ __ __ __

2. Argentina – A bread or pastry stuffed with meat, cheese or other ingredients, and then baked or fried * [ ) @ ? @ ^ @ __ __ __ __ __ __ __ __

3. Bolivia – A baked savoury pastry filled with beef, pork or chicken mixed in a sweet, slightly spicy or very spicy sauce / @ } ~ * ? @ /

   __ __ __ __ __ __ __ __

4. Peru – A dish made from fresh raw fish cured in citrus juices such as lemon or lime and spiced with chili peppers and additional seasonings % * ! " % = * __ __ __ __ __ __ __

5. Chile – A bread or pastry stuffed with meat, cheese or other ingredients, and then baked or fried * [ ) @ ? @ ^ @ __ __ __ __ __ __ __ __

6. Uruguay – Various meats cooked on a grill or an open fire – @ / @ ^ < –

   __ __ __ __ __

7. Ecuador – A fish soup cooked with onions * ? % * # < } } @ ^ <

   __ __ __ __ __ __ __ __ __ __ __

8. Paraguay – A spongy cake made of corn flour, cheese and milk or whey / <) @) @ > @ + | @ ` @ __ __ __ __ __ __ __ __ __ __ __ __ __

9. Suriname – A baked dish made of chicken, citrus juice and the root of the tayer plant (called 'pomtajer', and used as a replacement for potatoes)) < [__ __ __

10. Guyana – A stewed meat dish strongly flavoured with cinnamon, cassareep (a special sauce made from the cassava root), and other ingredients including Caribbean hot peppers) *)) * >) < ~ _ _ _ _ _ _ _ _ _

11. Venezuela – A plate of rice, shredded beef in stew and stewed black beans) @ # * } } < ? % > “ < } } < _ _ _ _ _ _ _ _ _ _ _ _ _ _ _

12. Colombia – Large pieces of meat, tubers and vegetables served in a broth / @ ? % < % = < _ _ _ _ _ _ _ _

116. WIDE-EYED WITH WONDER

Match the names of these South American natural wonders with what they are famous for.

Natural wonder	**What it is known for**
1. Atacama, Chile	a. A national park with daggers of mountain peaks and glacial lakes
2. Tierra del Fuego, Argentina	b. You can trek this glacier fed by the Southern Patagonian Ice Field
3. Galapagos Islands, Ecuador	c. This "Roof of the World" is the highest peak of the Andes
4. Salar de Uyuni, Bolivia	d. These 275 falls dwarf the Niagara Falls
5. Iguazu, Argentina/Brazil	e. The island's trees grow horizontally due to strong Antarctic winds
6. Torres del Paine, Chile	f. Gigantic lake, the world's highest navigable body of water
7. Colca, Peru	g. The world's driest desert includes coastal plains and volcanoes
8. Titicaca, Peru/Bolivia	h. Twice as deep as the Grand Canyon and full of Andean condors
9. Perito Moreno, Argentina	i. Its many endemic species influenced Darwin's theory of evolution
10. Aconcagua, Argentina	j. The world's largest salt flat is remarkable in the rainy season

117. SOMEWHAT FLUENT

Each letter group given below is contained in the name of a language spoken in South America. Can you identify these languages?

3-letter group	**Language**
EXAMPLE: SIA	**RUSSIAN**
1. ANI	________________
2. TUG	________________
3. GLI	________________
4. ARA	________________
5. ECH	________________
6. UTC	________________
7. MAR	________________

118. FLORAL PRO(CON)FUSION

Unscramble the flower names in the second column to identify the national flowers of the South American countries in the first column.

	Country	Scrambled Version	National Flower
1.	Guyana	ATREW YILL	_ _ _ _ _ _ _ _ _
2.	Colombia	SMARSHTIC DRICOH	_ _ _ _ _ _ _ _ _ _ _ _ _ _ _
3.	Venezuela	CHODIR	_ _ _ _ _ _
4.	Peru	ATTANKU	_ _ _ _ _ _ _
5.	Ecuador	ORES	_ _ _ _
6.	Uruguay	BOICE	_ _ _ _ _
7.	Chile	HILANCE WOLFREBELL	_ _ _ _ _ _ _ _ _ _ _ _ _ _ _ _ _
8.	Bolivia	UNAKTAT	_ _ _ _ _ _ _
9.	Argentina	OCEBI	_ _ _ _ _
10.	Brazil	LATECAYT HODIRC	_ _ _ _ _ _ _ _ _ _ _ _ _ _

119. MUSICAL EXCESSES

The name of each South American musical instrument contains a word that fits the clue in the second column. To find this word, cross off the extra letters in the name of the musical instrument and read the remaining letters from left to right. The country to which this dish belongs is given in brackets.

Musical Instrument		Clue	Answer
EXAMPLE:			
T R U ~~M P~~ E ~~T~~ (wind)		**Opposite of 'false'**	**T R U E**
1.	Culoepuya (Venezuela)	A sound made by a horse's hooves	________
2.	Oopoochawa (Uruguay)	An animal's foot	________
3.	Bahian guitar (Brazil)	A clue or suggestion	________
4.	Esterilla (Colombia)	Not moving	________
5.	Pinkillu (Bolivia)	A tablet, medicine	________
6.	Karawasi (Suriname)	Not cooked	________
7.	Rondador (Ecuador)	Sound made by a lion	________
8.	Yerbomatófono (Argentina)	You row it with oars	________
9.	Ajayu (Chile)	A type of bird	________
10.	Wakra phuku (Peru)	Cover or enclose, as in paper etc.	________

120. REVOLUTIONARY WORDS

Solve the clues and place one letter on each blank. Then insert the letters according to the numbers under them into the sentence below to arrive at a famous quote by revolutionary Che Guevara.

Specialised language used by a group : _ _ _ _ _ _
1 2 3 4 5 6

In a cunning manner : _ _ _ _ _ _ _ _
7 3 2 8 9 10 11 12

Made hot : _ _ _ _ _ _
13 2 3 14 15 16

Acts in a well-mannered way : _ _ _ _ _ _ _
17 15 18 2 19 15 20

"_ _ _ _ U _
10 8 12 5 9 3 15 14 17 11 15 13 10 9 18 10 6 16 10 4 6 2 9 10 5 9

_ _ _ _ _ _ _ _ _ _ U _ _ _ _ _ _ _ _ _ _ _ _ U
2 9 15 19 15 3 12 10 6 1 20 9 10 7 15 9 18 15 6 12 5

_ _ _ _ _ _ _ _ _ _ _ _ _ _ _ _ _ _ _."
2 3 15 2 7 5 14 3 2 16 15 5 9 14 10 6 15

ANSWERS

ASIA

1. HIDDEN CAPITALS

1. ChairMAN AMArillo – Manama, Bahrain
2. EricA, STAN, And – Astana, Kazakhstan
3. ToM, US, CATs – Muscat, Oman
4. AnushKA BULlies – Kabul, Afghanistan
5. MartHA, NO, I don't – HANOI, Vietnam
6. Jallianwala BAGH, DAD? – Baghdad, Iraq
7. MaDAM, AS CUStoms – Damascus, Syria
8. VincenT, ASH, KEN, Trent – Tashkent, Uzbekistan
9. OedeMA LE – Male, Maldives
10. PanaMA NIL And – Manila, The Philippines
11. DO HAbits – Doha, Qatar
12. EnriCO, LOMBOk is – Colombo, Sri Lanka

2. MONEY JOINS HANDS

1. Syria – Pound
2. Kyrgyzstan – Som
3. Laos – Kip
4. North Korea – Won
5. Myanmar – Kyat
6. Armenia – Dram
7 Kazakhstan – Tenge
8. Mongolia – Tugrik
9. Thailand – Baht
10. Tajikistan – Somoni
11. United Arab Emirates – Dirham
12. Vietnam – Dong

3. FLORAL BOUQUET

1. India – Lotus
2. Iraq – Rose
3. Vietnam – Red Lotus
4. Bhutan – Blue Poppy
5. Afghanistan – Tulip
6. North Korea – Magnolia
7. Nepal – Rhododendron
8. Israel – Cyclamen
9. Jordan – Black Iris
10. Syria – Jasmine

4. CHINESE RULE

S	R	G	Q	I	N	K	T	T
O	H	N	Y	I	M	G	L	D
A	Q	A	X	I	Q	Q	P	Y
I	P	T	N	I	S	O	N	G
L	K	G	N	G	Z	H	O	U
N	B	G	P	N	A	U	Y	X

Liao, Ming, Qin, Qing, Shang, Song, Tang, Xin, Yuan, Zhou

5. BEASTS OF PRIDE

1. East Timor – Crocodile
2. South Korea – Tiger
3. Japan – Pheasant
4. Lebanon – Phoenix
5. Nepal – Cow
6. Israel – Hoopoe
7. Qatar – Oryx
8. Laos – Elephant
9. Palestine – Sunbird
10. Cambodia – Giant Ibis

6. WHOSE BOOK IS IT?

1-d, 2-f, 3-a, 4-c, 5-h, 6-g, 7-b, 8-e

7. MY PIECE OF COUNTRY

1. Myanmar, 2. Singapore, 3. Taiwan, 4. Vietnam, 5. Yemen, 6. Lebanon, 7. Mongolia, 8. Kuwait, 9. Pakistan, 10. Bahrain, 11. Cambodia, 12. Bangladesh, 13. Indonesia, 14. The Philippines, 15. Turkmenistan

8. INCLUSIVE INVENTIONS

1. Off
2. Rain
3. Elm
4. Bus
5. Pure
6. Otter
7. Arms
8. Under
9. Late
10. Host
11. Rest
12. Gain

9. FIVE-LETTER CITIES

M	A	C	A	U	A	Y	Q
P	A	C	C	E	M	D	U
D	E	L	H	I	M	N	K
L	L	T	E	O	A	A	A
U	U	Z	R	N	N	K	B
O	S	A	K	A	T	A	U
E	O	O	N	H	A	H	L
S	M	C	I	T	P	D	Y

Amman, Delhi, Dhaka, Hanoi, Kabul, Kandy, Macau, Mecca, Mosul, Osaka, Patna, Petra, Seoul

10. LARGE DESERTS

Kayak, After, Road, Alter, Knee, Upper, Mile – Karakum Desert, Turkmenistan

Trunk, Amber, Knife, Llama, Angry, Meal, Apple, King, Ache, Nibble – Taklamakan, China

11. Booked!

1. And the Mountains Echoed – Khaled Hosseini – Afghanistan
2. The Good Earth – Pearl S Buck – China
3. Exodus – Leon Uris – Israel

4. Moth Smoke – Mohsin Hamid – Pakistan
5. Across the Nightingale Floor – Lian Hearn – Japan
6. Swami and Friends – R K Narayan – India
7. The Quiet American – Graham Greene – Vietnam
8. The Mountain is Young – Han Suyin – Nepal
9. A Golden Age – Tahmima Anam – Bangladesh
10. The Glass Palace – Amitav Ghosh – Myanmar

12. PRIZED PEOPLE

Michael Oondatje, Arundhati Roy, Salman Rushdie, Kazuo Ishiguro, Ruth Prawer Jhabvala
Turkish novelist Orhan Pamuk was awarded the Nobel prize for Literature in 2006.

13. ATOP THE MOUNTAIN

							M	A	K	A	L	U		
						N	O	S	H	A	Q			
						Y	U	S	H	A	N			
	D	A	M	A	V	A	N	D						
				L	H	O	T	S	E					
							F	A	N	S	I	P	A	N
	R	A	M	E	L	A	U							
K	A	N	C	H	E	N	J	U	N	G	A			
						K	I	N	A	B	A	L	U	

Mount Fuji is an active volcano in Japan.

14. RIVERS OF DELIGHT

1. Irrawaddy
2. Yangtze
3. Orontes
4. Brahmaputra
5. Indus
6. Mekong
7. Amu Darya
8. Euphrates

15. LEADING FROM THE FRONT

1-j, 2-g, 3-i, 4-h, 5-f, 6-k, 7-e, 8-l, 9-b, 10-a, 11-c, 12-d

16. LUSCIOUS LANGUAGES

1. Arabic, Burmese
2. Georgian, Hebrew (Israel)
3. Japanese, Khmer (Cambodia)
4. Malay, Lao
5. Nepali, Pashto (Afghanistan)
6. Persian, Portuguese
7. Sinhala, Uzbek
8. Kurdish, Filipino
9. Cantonese, Dzongkha
10. Urdu, Dari

17. COMFORT FOOD

1. Gay
2. Mob
3. Tab
4. Moo
5. Beak
6. Ump
7. Pour
8. Ran
9. Sang
10. Amen

18. WRITING IT UP

D	Y	N	C	I	A	M	A	R	A
E	E	K	A	L	P	L	M	G	Q
S	C	V	D	I	D	P	U	N	T
E	Y	T	A	R	G	R	J	I	B
N	R	I	N	N	M	R	B	N	C
I	I	M	D	U	A	E	O	I	V
L	L	D	K	D	T	G	B	E	K
A	L	H	K	A	I	A	A	A	G
B	I	T	N	D	R	S	N	R	D
R	C	P	N	A	Y	A	H	V	I

1. Arabic
2. Aramaic
3. Balinese
4. Cyrillic
5. Devanagari
6. Georgian
7. Gurmukhi
8. Kana
9. Tibetan
10. Yiddish

19. MOVIE MAGIC

1. Swayamvaram
2. Seven Samurai
3. Charulata
4. Chungking Express
5. Ugetsu
6. Sallah Shabati
7. Working Girls I
8. Bol
9. Muktir Gaan
10. A Time To Live, A Time to Die
11. Where is Friend's Home?

20. WORDS TO LIVE BY

We can never obtain peace in the outer world until we make peace with ourselves.

AFRICA

21. WHERE AM I?

1. Malawi: Listen, MA, LAW Is the only thing I want to study.
2. Congo: Is this BaCON GOing bad?
3. Lesotho: He knows how to juggLE SO THOroughly that ...
4. Uganda: this rUG AND A footstool ...
5. Eritrea: I gathER IT REAssures you ...
6. Algeria: We have speciAL GERIAtric facilities ...

7. Chad: The coaCH ADdressed ...
8. Benin: ... this viBE NINe days ago ...
9. Togo: I want TO GO to Africa.
10. Rwanda: SlendeR, WAN DAmsel, this ...

22. MUDDLED RIVERS

1. Limpopo, South Africa
2. Orange, Lesotho
3. Zambezi, Zambia
4. Okavango, Angola
5. Senegal, Guinea
6. Volta, Ghana
7. Niger, Guinea
8. Blue Nile, Ethiopia

23. ADDING LANGUAGES

Hausa, Berber, Nubian, Maasai, Yoruba, Ashanti, Igbo, Kirundi, Malagasy, Xhosa, Zulu, Ndebele.

24. PARK IT HERE

Bin, Hoe, Wag, Leak, Band, Noon, Thaw, Mink

25. A BIRD BY ANOTHER NAME

1. Golden Eagle
2. Garden Bulbul
3. Grey-headed Kingfisher
4. Dodo
5. Secretary Bird
6. African Fish Eagle
7. Blue Crane
8. Red-crested Turaco
9. White-cheeked Turaco
10. Black-crowned Crane
11. Purple-crested Turaco
12. Lilac-breasted Roller

Namibia, South Sudan, Zambia, Zimbabwe

26. ANIMALS ACROSS AFRICA

27. PRECIOUS RESERVES

															S	O	U	T	H	A	F	R	I	C	A
													A	L	G	E	R	I	A						
														M	A	L	A	W	I						
													G	A	B	O	N								
														N	A	M	I	B	I	A					
C	E	N	T	R	A	L	A	F	R	I	C	A	N	R	E	P	U	B	L	I	C				
															Z	A	M	B	I	A					

28. MINER-AL-PHABET

1. Bauxite
2. Cobalt
3. Chromite
4. Manganese
5. Uranium
6. Gold
7. Nickel
8. Petroleum
9. Gypsum
10. Phosphorite
11. Vanadium
12. Tungsten
13. Diamonds
14. Wolframite
15. Talc
16. Titanium Ore
17. Aluminium
18. Platinum
19. Copper
20. Asbestos
21. Lithium
22. Fluorite
23. Zinc
24. Iron Ore

29. CAPITAL FRAGMENTS

1. MogaDIShu, Somalia
2. BuJUMbura, Burundi
3. AntaNANarivo, Madagascar
4. KIGAli, Rwanda
5. TUNIs, Tunisia
6. RABAt, Morocco
7. MAPUto, Mozambique
8. DODOma, Tanzania
9. JUBA, South Sudan
10. LUANda, Angola
11. LiBREville, Gabon
12. WinDHOek, Namibia
13. PRAIa, Cape Verde
14. MonROVia, Liberia
15. AcCRA, Ghana
16. PoRT Louis, Mauritius
17. Ouagadougou, Burkina Faso
18. KamPALa, Uganda
19. ViCTOria, Seychelles
20. AddiS ABaba, Ethiopia

30. WHO AM I?

1. South Sudan
2. Zambia
3. Malawi
4. Uganda
5. Rwanda
6. Lesotho

31. RENAMED

1-g, 2-e, 3-i, 4-j, 5-d, 6-a, 7-m, 8-f, 9-n, 10-c, 11-l, 12-o, 13-k, 14-b, 15-h

32. MYSTERY ISLE

Comoros
Madagascar
São Tomé and Príncipe
Seychelles
Cape Verde
Mauritius

33. CURRENCY ISSUES

1. Angola – Kwanza
2. Mauritania – Ouguiya
3. Swaziland – Lilangeni
4. São Tomé and Príncipe – Dobra
5. Ghana – Cedi
6. Nigeria – Naira
7. Ethiopia – Birr
8. Botswana – Pula
9. Eritrea – Nakfa
10. Madagascar – Malagasy Ariary
11. South Africa – Rand
12. Lesotho – Loti
13. Mozambique – Metical
14. Cape Verde – Escudo
15. Gambia – Dalasi

34. AFRICAN ADVENTURES

1. King Solomon's Mines
2. Heart of Darkness
3. Tarzan of the Apes
4. The Story of Doctor Dolittle
5. Five Weeks in a Balloon
6. Elephant Song
7. The Gorilla Hunters
8. The Dogs of War
9. Cross Country
10. Juggernaut

35. PEACE BE TO ALL!

1. Anwar El Sadat
2. Desmond Tutu
3. Ellen Johnson Sirleaf
4. Nelson Mandela
5. Wangari Muta Maathai
6. Mohamed ElBaradei
7. Leymah Gbowee

36. JUST DESERTS

A	B	A	B	A	N	E	D	A	G	O	O	R	A	K	N
R	A	V	I	Y	I	L	P	R	F	Y	B	E	B	A	R
A	L	B	I	S	Y	F	L	A	L	E	A	L	M	L	T
B	I	R	S	H	T	U	M	H	O	L	I	I	L	A	E
D	I	T	O	N	O	R	A	A	W	I	B	L	A	H	C
N	R	H	A	P	H	R	T	S	S	M	R	A	N	A	T
A	G	B	M	O	C	A	M	E	D	E	S	B	O	R	C
R	U	O	L	A	V	A	B	O	D	A	N	A	K	I	L
G	L	A	T	S	A	O	C	N	A	E	R	T	I	R	E

Chalbi, Danakil, Eritrean coastal, Grand Bara, Guban, Kalahari, Karoo, Lompoul, Moçâmedes, Namib, Nyiri, Ogaden, Sahara. The Sahara, Africa's largest desert and the world's largest hot desert, itself comprises many different deserts.

37. DANCING THE NIGHT AWAY

1	2	3	4	5	6	7
S	**O**	**U**	**K**	**O**	**U**	**S**
E	D	P	O	R	N	A
S	I	L	U	G	J	L
A	O	I	R	A	U	I
M	U	N	O	N	S	V
E	**S**	**K**	**I**	**S**	**T**	**A**

National Dance of the Democratic Republic of the Congo – SOUKOUS

National Dance of Ethiopia – ESKISTA

38. JUST LIKE AN EGYPTIAN

1. Pharaoh 2. Pyramid 3. Papyrus 4. Scribe 5. Obelisk
6. Hieroglyph 7. Sphinx 8. Scarab 9. Ankh 10. Mummy

39. FAMOUS SAYING

Morning, Study, Flew, Chapters

'Education is the most powerful weapon which you can use to change the world.' ~ Nelson Mandela

40. GEOGRAPHICAL ODDITIES

1. Gabon – The other countries form the region called the Horn of Africa.
2. Senegal – The Atlas mountain range extends across the other countries.
3. Namibia – The other countries constitute the Great Rift Valley.
4. Zambia – The Tropic of Capricorn passes through the other countries.
5. Kenya – Parts of the other countries form the Kalahari Desert.
6. Angola – The other countries form part of the Sahel, the savanna that separates the Sahara desert from the more fertile regions in the South.
7. Sierra Leone – The other countries form part of the Sahara Desert.
8. Central African Republic – The other countries form part of the South African plateau.
9. Somalia – The other countries form part of the Congo Basin.
10. Cameroon – The Tropic of Cancer passes through the other countries.

AUSTRALIA / OCEANIA / ANTARCTICA

41. COUNTRIFIED

1. ... suFI JIggled... 2. ... contesSA MOAn... 3. ... tuTU VALUed...
4. ... ChiNA, URUguay... 5. ... HaraKIRI BATIked". 6. ... princiPAL AUditor...
7. ... skeleTON GAllery...

42. CAPITAL GAME

1-m, 2-k, 3-l, 4-i, 5-a, 6-j, 7-b, 8-d, 9-f, 10-n, 11-h, 12-g, 13-c, 14-e

43. POCKETING THE MARSUPIALS

		G	L	I	D	E	R						
				A	N	T	E	C	H	I	N	U	S
					P	A	D	E	M	E	L	O	N
				Q	U	O	K	K	A				
T	A	S	M	A	N	I	A	N	D	E	V	I	L
		B	E	T	T	O	N	G					
				M	U	L	G	A	R	A			
			W	A	L	L	A	B	Y				
		W	A	L	L	A	R	O	O				
	B	A	N	D	I	C	O	O	T				
						K	O	A	L	A			
		W	O	Y	L	I	E						
					N	U	M	B	A	T			
						Q	U	O	L	L			

The national animal of Australia is the red kangaroo, and its national bird is the emu.

44. IT DEPENDS

F	R	E	N	C	H	P	O	L	Y	N	E	S	I	A
C	N	O	R	F	O	L	K	I	S	L	A	N	D	N
J	U	Z	A	S	P	R	F	T	G	I	V	B	Z	U
G	A	A	O	T	R	W	S	E	N	A	E	V	A	T
K	T	L	M	R	E	E	E	O	Q	U	O	L	R	U
K	W	A	A	E	L	A	D	R	O	T	E	Y	R	F
Y	R	M	S	W	T	E	O	L	O	K	U	I	U	D
H	T	P	N	D	L	D	U	N	O	S	P	R	Y	N
I	H	S	A	A	F	G	F	T	M	F	Y	A	N	A
P	I	T	C	A	I	R	N	I	S	L	A	N	D	S
I	H	W	I	P	E	P	L	A	T	E	R	E	S	I
I	E	T	R	A	Q	U	D	E	D	W	S	T	Y	L
N	F	K	E	E	I	E	I	U	O	M	M	K	J	L
I	R	T	M	P	L	T	X	N	A	I	E	E	W	A
E	P	S	A	R	D	N	A	L	S	I	E	K	A	W

45. PEEK-A-BOO!

1. Hobart
2. Cairns
3. Perth
4. Brisbane
5. Darwin
6. Ballarat

7. Adelaide
8. Sydney
9. Melbourne
10. Canberra
11. Dunedin
12. Auckland
13. Christchurch
14. Wellington
15. Invercargill

Cities from 1 – 10 are in Australia, while the others are in New Zealand.

46. (F) ANTARCTIC ANIMALS

1. Blue-eyed shag
2. Emperor Penguin
3. Giant petrel
4. Leopard Seal
5. Crabeater Seal
6. Krill
7. Arctic Tern
8. Cape Pigeon
9. Snowy Sheathbill
10. Snow Petrel
11. Antarctic Skua
12. Southern Fur Seal
13. King Penguin
14. Wandering Albatross

47. ATTENTION, FILM-GOERS!

1. Russell Crowe
2. Cate Blanchett
3. Lucy Lawless
4. Sam Worthington
5. Naomi Watts
6. Geoffrey Rush
7. Nicole Kidman
8. Radha Mitchell
9. Hugh Jackman
10. Heath Ledger

48. OCCUPATIONAL HAZARD

1-h, 2-k, 3-f, 4-l, 5-a, 6-j, 7-n, 8-b, 9-o, 10-c, 11-d, 12-m, 13-e, 14-i, 15-g

49. BOOK IT!

1. Thomas Keneally
2. Keri Hulme
3. Peter Carey
4. DBC Pierre
5. Eleanor Catton
6. Richard Flanagan

50. QUIET FLOWS THE RIVER

1. Dreketi, Fiji
2. Papenoo, French Polynesia
3. Kabenau, Papua New Guinea
4. Murray, Australia
5. Avana, Cook Islands
6. Murrumbidgee, Australia
7. Darling, Australia
8. Waikato, New Zealand
9. Clarence, New Zealand
10. Derwent, Australia
11. Navua, Fiji
12. Fly, Papua New Guinea

51. HERITAGE BOX

1. Shark Bay
2. Rock Islands
3. Kuk Swamp
4. East Rennell, Solomon Islands
5. Great Barrier Reef, Aus
6. Bikini Atoll, Marshall

7. Fraser Island, Aus
8. Tongariro, NZ
9. Chief Roi Mata's Domain, Vanuatu
10. Te Wahipounamu, NZ
11. Henderson, Pitcairn Islands
12. Levuka, Fiji
13. Phoenix Islands, Kiribati

52. IDENTITY CRISIS

1. Adam Gilchrist, Brendan McCullum
2. Richard Hadlee, Dennis Lillee
3. Ricky Ponting, Ross Taylor
4. Shane Warne, David Warner
5. Martin Guptill, Michael Clarke
6. Glenn McGrath, Brett Lee
7. Brad Hogg, Adam Miller
8. Mark Gillespie, Daniel Vettori
9. Michael Hussey, Cameron White
10. Steve Waugh, Mark Taylor

53. CAN-BERRA?

							W	E	S	T	O	N	I	A	
				W	A	R	O	O	K	A					
			W	I	L	M	O	T							
		W	H	Y	A	L	L	A							
		W	A	L	L	A	W	A	L	L	A				
			W	O	N	T	H	A	G	G	I				
			W	O	M	B	E	Y	A	N	C	A	V	E	S
						W	A	R	M	U	N				
W	A	N	G	A	R	A	T	T	A						
			W	Y	O	N	G								
				W	A	R	O	O	N	A					
				W	O	O	L	I							
					W	U	D	I	N	N	A				

Since there was so much wool, wheat and gold in Australia, there was actually a suggestion that the capital be called Woolwheatgold!

54. MAORI CULTURE

1. Terms, Te Reo
2. Pakoras, Pakeha
3. Marks, Marae
4. Mango, Manaakitanga
5. Hakka, Haka
6. Powerful, Powhiri
7. Whale, Whaikōrero
8. Kappa, Kapa haka
9. Honey, Hongi

55. FLYING OVER THE WATER

Cockatoo, Raven, Cassowary, Magpie, Kookaburra, Heron, Ibis, Lorikeet, Platypus

TASMAN SEA

EUROPE

56. LOST IN URBAN SPACES

1. Berlin 2. Paris 3. Kiev 4. Minsk 5. Sofia
6. Odessa 7. Rome 8. Istanbul 9. London 10. Milan

57. FRAGMENTED COAST

1. Edinburgh 2. Venice 3. Istanbul 4. Oslo
5. Lisbon 6. Helsinki 7. Dublin 8. Copenhagen
9. Barcelona 10. Dubrovnik 11. Genoa 12. Marseilles

58. MIXED BORDERS

1. Cyprus, Belarus 2. Portugal, San Marino 3. Albania, Andorra
4. Macedonia, Montenegro 5. Croatia, Sweden 6. Estonia, Greece
7. Denmark, Germany 8. Finland, Lithuania 9. Armenia, Slovakia
10. Kosovo, Poland 11. Luxembourg, Netherlands 12. Monaco, Malta

59. STARRING CITIES

			G	A	B	R	O	V	O
			S	H	U	M	E	N	
Y	A	M	B	O	L				
		B	U	R	G	A	S		
					A	Y	T	O	S
				V	R	A	T	S	A
	P	E	R	N	I	K			
	T	R	O	Y	A	N			

60. ADD CHEESE FOR FLAVOUR

1. Gruyere 2. Emmental 3. Fondue 4. Raclette
5. Ricotta 6. Cheddar 7. Mascarpone 8. Camembert
9. Stilton 10. Munster 11. Roquefort 12. Halloumi
13. Havarti 14. Mimolette 15. Gorgonzola

61. JUMBLED BRUSHES

1. Paul Cezanne 2. Joan Miro 3. Paul Gauguin 4. Edouard Manet
5. Edgar Degas 6. Claude Monet 7. Raphael 8. El Greco
9. Michaelangelo 10. Salvador Dali

62. LOST IN THE MARKET

J	M	M	T	A	I	F	J	T	G	M
P	E	U	G	E	O	T	F	I	A	T
T	N	S	E	D	E	C	R	E	M	P
B	I	E	Z	I	A	S	G	D	O	K
E	R	W	O	U	R	V	K	R	Q	A
N	A	A	D	R	O	A	S	O	I	D
T	R	I	U	L	T	C	R	C	D	O
L	R	T	V	G	H	I	A	R	P	A
E	E	O	D	E	A	D	C	E	E	L
Y	F	N	J	B	Z	J	L	K	K	F

1. Mercedes
2. Audi
3. Porsche
4. Opel
5. Bentley
6. Jaguar
7. Volvo
8. Dacia
9. Fiat
10. Ferrari
11. Peugeot
12. Citroen

63. PROTECT THE RIGHT ONE

1-o, 2-n, 3-l, 4-i, 5-h, 6-a, 7-j, 8-c, 9-m, 10-d, 11-g, 12-b, 13-f, 14-k, 15-e

64. MAKING MUSIC

1. Clarinet
2. Trombone
3. Bassoon
4. Timpani
5. Vibraphone
6. Cymbals
7. Trumpet
8. Saxophone
9. Violin
10. Piccolo
11. Tuba
12. Triangle
13. Piano
14. Oboe
15. Flute

65. LINGUISTIC FERVOUR

1. Candy (Persian)
2. Macramé (Arabic)
3. Beryl (Sanskrit)
4. Sorbet (Hindustani)
5. Cheroot (Tamil)
6. Ketchup (Chinese)
7. Person (Etruscan)
8. Junk (Indonesian)
9. Glitch (Yiddish)
10. Gingham (Malay)

66. DAHL'S CHICKENS

1. The Magic Finger
2. Fantastic Mr Fox
3. James and the Giant Peach
4. Charlie and the Chocolate Factory
5. Matilda
6. The BFG
7. The Twits
8. The Witches
9. George's Marvellous Medicine
10. Danny, The Champion of the World

11. Boy: Tales of Childhood
12. The Gremlins
13. Dirty Beasts
14. Going Solo
15. Esio Trot

67. FITTING THE ROLE

1-g, 2-e, 3-i, 4-j, 5-d, 6-a, 7-m, 8-f, 9-n, 10-c, 11-l, 12-o, 13-k, 14-b, 15-h

68. Crossing Towns

				N					O				
				A	R	A	D		R				
				V					A	D	J	U	D
				O					S				
				D			I		T				
			M	A	N	G	A	L	I	A			
				R			S		E				
R	E	G	H	I	N		I						

These towns are in Romania.

69. LOOKING FOR A COUNTRY

L	O	H	N	S	F	E	L	D	N	P
	K	(G)	(E)	M	E	X	U	L	H	O
C	C	E	S	E	E	L	(R)	A	A	O
H	E	L	A	B	E	N	Z	N	S	L
T	L	I	R	S	T	A	L	G	N	O
E	A	N	G	U	A	L	A	E	E	S
Z	T	I	W	A	L	Y	M	N	L	S
L	A	U	T	R	A	C	H	T	O	A
L	I	N	D	O	W	H	(M)	H	O	T
(A)	L	A	N	Z	(N)	E	(Y)	A	F	A
T	T	I	W	E	D	N	I	L	T	L

These towns are in Germany.

70. TRIBAL ROOTS

1. Ace, Pan, Ash, Asp, Hid – CASSI
2. One, Far, Bud, Ant, Tee, Use – NAUNES
3. Mat, Ire, Eve, Red, Arc, Ink, Tin – ARVERNI
4. All, Dad, Apt, Tie, Ice, Did, End, Fit - LAPICINI

71. VISITING THE RIVIERA

1. Vistula
2. Tagus
3. Loire
4. Meuse
5. Oder
6. Dneiper
7. Danube
8. Ural
9. Volga
10. Rhine
11. Elbe
12. Rhone
13. Seine
14. Moselle
15. Thames

72. REMEMBERING RHYMES

1. Wall
2. Wool
3. Diamond
4. Hill
5. Pieman
6. Roses
7. Mulberry bush
8. Mouse
9. Tuffet
10. Farmer's wife
11. Lamb
12. Sheep

73. MISSING SCIENTISTS

1. Albert Einstein
2. Charles Darwin
3. Archimedes
4. Copernicus
5. Isaac Newton
6. Marie Curie
7. Leonardo da Vinci
8. Galileo
9. Aristotle
10. Louis Pasteur

74. POLL-IT-I(C)S

75. LET THERE BE PEACE!

1. Poland, Lech Walesa
2. Finland, Martti Ahtisaari
3. Ireland, John Hume
4. United Kingdom, Betty Williams
5. France, Rene Cassin
6. Belgium, Dominique Pire
7. Sweden, Alva Myrdal

NORTH AMERICA

76. PITA IN THE CAPITAL

1. St. George's – Grenada
2. Port–au–Prince – Haiti
3. Port of Spain – Trinidad and Tobago
4. Kingston – Jamaica
5. Managua – Nicaragua
6. Bridgetown – Barbados
7. Havana – Cuba
8. Nassau – Bahamas
9. Panama City – Panama
10. San Jose – Costa Rica

77. COLD WORDS

K	A	T	I	Y	A	N	A	T
N	A	P	S	N	O	K	B	A
I	I	Y	U	M	R	I	L	Y
L	C	L	A	I	N	Y	U	N
T	T	L	K	Y	H	N	W	I
A	T	A	I	A	N	C	I	L
H	Y	O	W	M	N	I	D	O
A	T	A	L	I	N	I	Q	R
H	T	L	A	L	M	A	N	E
C	A	N	A	L	T	N	E	M

Snow – All these are words for different types of snow.

78. STATING THE OBVIOUS

1. Illinois, Colorado
2. Utah, Iowa
3. Maryland, Virginia
4. Oregon, Kansas
5. Missouri, Wisconsin
6. Pennsylvania, Connecticut
7. Louisiana, Tennessee
8. Arizona, Nevada
9. Alaska, Montana
10. Nebraska, Arkansas

79. STATES OF MYSTERY

C	O	L	I	M	A				
	M	O	R	E	L	O	S		
	T	L	A	X	C	A	L	A	
			H	I	D	A	L	G	O
O	A	X	A	C	A				
	S	O	N	O	R	A			

80. MONEY MATCH

1-f-vi, 2-e-v, 3-g-(any from i. to iv.), 4-a-(any from i. to iv.), 5-b-(any from i. to iv.), 6-c-vii, 7-d-(any from i. to iv.)

81. CARTOON CHARACTERS

1. Bruce Wayne
2. Captain K'nuckles
3. Emily Elizabeth
4. Timmy Turner
5. Boots
6. Miranda Isabella Sanchez
7. Tino Tonitini
8. Shego
9. Nigel Uno
10. Uncle Rico

82. EMBLEMATIC PRIDE

1. Saint Lucia
2. Mexico
3. Belize
4. Saint Vincent and the Grenadines
5. Antigua and Barbuda
6. Dominican Republic
7. Canada
8. Trinidad and Tobago
9. Guatemala
10. Barbados
11. Jamaica
12. The Bahamas

83. ROUTE IT THIS WAY

1. Newport
2. Albany
3. Caldwell
4. Sioux City
5. Rockford
6. Chicago
7. Cleveland
8. Buffalo
9. Springfield
10. Waltham

84. ADDING UP TO IT

1. Castries
2. Tegucigalpa
3. Roseau
4. Saint John's
5. Basseterre
6. Ottawa
7. Belmopan
8. Santo Domingo

85. MAKE A MATCH

1-g, 2-d, 3-a, 4-f, 5-b, 6-c, 7-e.

86. ISLAND FUN

1. Maui, 2. Ni'ihau, 3. Kaua'i, 4. O'ahu, 5. Lana'i, 6. Moloka'i, 7. Kaho'olawe.

The eighth island and the group of islands are both called **Hawaii**.

87. ENDANGERED AND MISSING

1. Zempoaltepec Vole
2. Brown's Hutia
3. Vaquita
4. Hawaiian Hoary Bat
5. Roatan Island Agouti
6. Haitian Solenodon
7. Jaguarundi
8. San Joaquin Kit Fox
9. Woodland caribou
10. Yucatan Brown Brocket Deer
11. Vancouver Island Marmot
12. Pronghorn
13. Buller's Chipmunk

88. POINTING UP

1. Pico Duarte
2. Pic la Selle
3. Blue Mountain Peak
4. Pico Turquino
5. Morne Diablotins
6. La Soufriere
7. Mount Liamuiga
8. Denali
9. Mount Logan
10. Popocatepetl

89. NAME THE PARK

1. Elle / Levera
2. Catherine / Negril
3. Louis / Isla Cabritos
4. Rebecca / Caguanes
5. Trish / Shenandoah
6. Oscar / Arrecife Alacranes
7. Jerome / Melajo
8. Mitch / Chagres
9. Colin / Inagua
10. Khadija / Jasper
11. Louise / Selva Negra
12. Lionel / El Rosario

90. JUMBLED HEADS

1. George Washington
2. Thomas Jefferson
3. Abraham Lincoln
4. Woodrow Wilson
5. John Kennedy
6. Dwight Eisenhower
7. William Clinton
8. Franklin Roosevelt
9. John Adams
10. Harry Truman

91. NOBLE IS AS NOBEL DOES

1-h-ii, 2-d-viii, 3-a-x, 4-g-iv, 5-j-v, 6-k-iii, 7-b-ix, 8-l-vii, 9-e-vi, 10-o-xi, 11-c-xv, 12-n-i, 13-f-xiv, 14-i-xii, 15-m-xiii

92. CLASSIC AMERICANA

1. John Steinbeck
2. Alice Walker
3. Jack Kerouac
4. Harper Lee
5. Kurt Vonnegut
6. Henry James
7. Mark Twain
8. Ayn Rand
9. Ray Bradbury
10. Arthur Miller
11. Toni Morrison
12. Maya Angelou
13. Harriet Beecher Stowe
14. Ernest Hemingway
15. Nathaniel Hawthorne

93. SHE'S SIMPLY THE BEST!

N	I	C	O	L	E	K	I	D	M	A	N		
S	U	S	A	N	S	A	R	A	N	D	O	N	
M	E	R	Y	L	S	T	R	E	E	P			
	E	M	M	A	T	H	O	M	P	S	O	N	
		J	U	L	I	A	R	O	B	E	R	T	S
		H	I	L	A	R	Y	S	W	A	N	K	
			J	O	D	I	E	F	O	S	T	E	R
	V	I	V	I	E	N	L	E	I	G	H		
		J	U	L	I	E	A	N	D	R	E	W	S
			S	O	P	H	I	A	L	O	R	E	N
			K	A	T	E	W	I	N	S	L	E	T
S	I	S	S	Y	S	P	A	C	E	K			
	H	A	L	L	E	B	E	R	R	Y			
H	O	L	L	Y	H	U	N	T	E	R			
B	R	I	E	L	A	R	S	O	N				
		H	E	L	E	N	M	I	R	R	E	N	

Katharine Hepburn has four Academy Awards, the maximum anyone has won as Best Actress in a Leading Role. She won them for her roles in *Morning Glory* (1933), *Guess Who's Coming to Dinner* (1967), *The Lion in Winter* (1968), *On Golden Pond* (1981).

94. WHAT'S IN THE RIVER?

1. Rich
2. Mail
3. Gland
4. Tense
5. Mate
6. Moo
7. Plot
8. Snap
9. Rare
10. Clove
11. Cost
12. Crash

95. DOT WHAT?

1-d, 2-n, 3-k, 4-p, 5-m, 6-r, 7-c, 8-q, 9-j, 10-s, 11-t, 12-i, 13-a, 14-b, 15-h, 16-f, 17-l, 18-o, 19-e, 20-g

96. TRIBAL WISDOM

Wrestle, Knowledge, Family, Punch.

"If we wonder often, the gift of knowledge will come." ~ Arapaho

"One finger cannot lift a pebble." ~ Hopi

"Don't let yesterday use up too much of today." ~ Cherokee

97. WHO RUN THE WORLD? GIRLS!

1-g, 2-i, 3-e, 4-h, 5-j, 6-b, 7-c, 8-f, 9-a, 10-d

98. TESTING TIMES

N	E	A	R	L	Y	P	O	~~A~~	~~L~~	~~L~~	C
X	~~M~~	~~E~~	~~N~~	D	U	N	~~C~~	~~A~~	~~N~~	C	O
O	L	I	N	~~S~~	~~T~~	~~A~~	~~N~~	~~D~~	R	I	M
D	A	~~A~~	~~D~~	~~V~~	~~E~~	~~R~~	~~S~~	~~I~~	~~T~~	~~Y~~	B
~~B~~	~~U~~	~~T~~	A	~~I~~	~~F~~	F	O	T	~~Y~~	~~O~~	~~U~~
R	~~W~~	~~A~~	~~N~~	~~T~~	B	I	~~T~~	~~O~~	B	Y	E
~~T~~	~~E~~	~~S~~	~~T~~	L	A	S	~~A~~	~~M~~	~~A~~	~~N~~	~~S~~
~~C~~	~~H~~	~~A~~	~~R~~	~~A~~	~~C~~	~~T~~	~~E~~	~~R~~	P	E	R
~~G~~	~~I~~	~~V~~	~~E~~	S	U	M	~~H~~	~~I~~	~~M~~	E	T
I	S	S	T	O	~~P~~	~~O~~	~~W~~	~~E~~	~~R~~	L	A

Nearly all men can stand adversity, but if you want to test a man's character, give him power.

99. MUSICAL MATCH

1-c, 2-e, 3-g (or d), 4-a, 5-i, 6-b, 7-j, 8-d (or g), 9-h, 10-f

100. GOLDEN WORDS

"The time is always right to do what is right."

SOUTH AMERICA

101. MASKED COUNTRY

1. Chile – ... hibaCHI LEts you...
2. Guyana – ... a GUY ANAlyse...
3. Peru – ... anteloPE RUbbed...
4. Suriname – ... tiramiSU, RINA, MElts...
5. Bolivia – GraB OLIVIA...
6. Brazil – ... algeBRA ZILlions...
7. Argentina – VulgAR GENT IN A...
8. Colombia – ... COL. OM BIAnnual...

102. CITIES MAKE A COUNTRY

	C	U	R	I	T	I	B	A		
			L	O	N	D	R	I	N	A
				M	A	N	A	U	S	
F	O	R	T	A	L	E	Z	A		
				R	E	C	I	F	E	
			N	A	T	A	L			

103. CAPITAL CHAOS

N	R	S	V	A	N	P	C	L	O
O	W	M	A	N	T	A	Q	E	Z
	M	O	J	N	Y	O	D	R	S
C	Y	Z	T	E	T	I	G	A	D
N	R	E	N	E	V	I	C	O	J
U	L	N	L	E	G	A	A	Q	B
S	E	I	T	N	R	R	U	G	D
A	L	N	M	A	A	I	O	B	O
K	O	R	C	A	T	T	R	E	D
M	R	K	L	O	L	T	S	T	G

1. Venezuela
2. Ecuador
3. Guyana
4. Paraguay
5. Chile
6. Falkland Islands
7. Peru
8. Colombia
9. French Guiana
10. Uruguay

104. FOUND ONLY HERE

1. Giant Tortoise
2. Anaconda
3. Southern Right Whale
4. Capybara
5. Andean Condor
6. Marine Iguana
7. Flightless Cormorant
8. Galapagos Finches
9. Galapagos Penguins
10. Magnificent Frigatebird
11. Large Painted Locusts
12. Golden Lion Tamarin

105. JUMBLED, PRIZED BOOKS

1. Pablo Neruda
2. Gabriela Mistral
3. Mario Vargas Llosa
4. Gabriel Garcia Marquez

106. THE AWE-INSPRING INCAS

Alligator, Turkey, Ant, Horse, Umbrellabird, Aardvark, Lobster, Pigeon, Armadillo – ATAHUALPA (The last emperor of the Incas)

Vulture, Ibis, Ram, Albatross, Civet, Owl, Cougar, Hyena, Anteater – VIRACOCHA (The Inca deity who is believed to have created all living things. He is also known as Pachacamac.

107. TRIBAL GAPS

Yanked, Yanomami
Queue, Quechua
Piano, Piaroa
Palm, Palikur
Table, Tabahara
Tsarina, Tsachila
Amazing, Amaicha
Change, Chango
Barber, Bara
Mackerel, Machiguenga
Villain, Vilela
Sand, Sanapana
Length, Lengua

108. LIFE-GIVING WATERS

1. Adopts 2. Malady 3. Adorns 4. Zenana 5. Orange 6. Nomads

The rivers are Amazon and Parana.

109. MOVE TO THE BEAT

			C	H	A	M	A	M	E				
C	H	A	C	A	R	E	R	A					
		M	U	R	G	A							
			C	U	E	C	A						
		C	A	R	N	A	V	A	L	I	T	O	
	C	U	A	R	T	E	T	O					
	C	U	M	B	I	A	V	I	L	L	E	R	A
			T	A	N	G	O						
				Z	A	M	B	A					

110. FAME IS WHAT FAME DOES

1-Colombia-xii, 2-n-viii, 3-f-x, 4-a-ix, 5Argentinal-ii, 6-j-xiv, 7-m-iv, 8-d-i, 9-b-v, 10-c-xv, 11-Brazil-vi, 12-o-vii, 13-Argentina-xiii, 14-Brazil-iii, 15-Colombia-xi

111. RI-O-LYMPICS

1. Kosovo, South Sudan, The Refugee Olympic Team
2. Rio de Janeiro, Sao Paulo, Salvador, Brasilia, Manaus
3. Maracana Stadium
4. Vinicius, combining aspects of Brazilian wildlife
5. Live your passion
6. Golf (returned after 112 years) and rugby (returned after 92 years)
7. Brazilian footballer Pele
8. Pierre de Coubertin medal for sportsmanship
9. Michael Phelps won 6 medals (five gold and one silver) for swimming
10. Zika virus

112. HOW RESOURCEFUL!

1. Colombia, coal
2. Brazil, iron ore
3. Chile, molybdenum
4. Peru, copper
5. Bolivia, tin
6. Guyana, bauxite
7. Argentina, limestone
8. Uruguay, marble
9. Bolivia, manganese
10. Peru, silver

113. COMPREENDO PORTUGUESE

1. Yes
2. Water
3. Body
4. Nurse
5. Clock
6. Do
7. Far
8. Good
9. Beautiful
10. Never
11. Time
12. Day
13. Life
14. Excuse me
15. Thank you

114. PROTECTING THE ENDANGERED

B	G	O	L	D	E	N	L	I	O	N	T	A	M	A	R	I	N
G	R	H	Y	A	C	I	N	T	H	M	A	C	A	W	B	M	K
O	G	O	H	T	O	L	S	D	E	O	T	L	E	E	R	H	T
R	I	W	W	K	N	M	R	J	T	X	L	L	T	B	T	M	G
F	A	P	N	N	V	I	Q	E	Y	B	G	X	L	P	O	W	B
T	N	X	Y	T	S	M	H	P	T	A	M	U	K	U	J	Y	M
R	T	L	Q	G	G	P	Y	P	E	T	E	Q	N	Y	B	W	N
A	A	B	E	L	M	B	I	Y	L	P	O	T	W	X	T	W	M
D	R	Y	Z	A	L	Y	P	D	O	O	A	T	T	M	T	M	Y
N	M	K	R	Y	R	R	M	I	E	I	D	W	N	L	X	Q	M
O	A	V	M	A	A	S	S	A	V	R	X	K	P	A	Y	V	D
S	D	Z	B	H	U	O	M	T	R	T	M	Y	N	L	I	B	Y
I	I	Q	D	B	N	G	A	A	G	M	X	O	G	I	Q	G	R
O	L	B	R	F	M	P	A	K	C	K	O	R	N	J	P	P	L
P	L	L	R	Q	I	N	R	J	R	A	J	S	Y	K	V	D	N
Y	O	O	B	R	Q	T	J	Y	Z	R	W	Q	E	R	E	T	R
D	G	Q	Y	R	Z	T	Y	M	Z	R	M	N	J	T	G	Y	D

115. UNLOCK THE FLAVOURS

1. Feijoada
2. Empanada
3. Saltenas
4. Ceviche
5. Asado
6. Encebollado
7. Sopa paraguaya
8. Pom
9. Pepperpot
10. Pabellon Criollo
11. Sancocho

116. WIDE-EYED WITH WONDER

1-g, 2-e, 3-i, 4-j, 5-d, 6-a, 7-h, 8-f, 9-b, 10-c

117. SOMEWHAT FLUENT

1. Spanish (most countries)
2. Portuguese (Brazil)
3. English (Guyana)
4. Guarani (Paraguay)
5. Quechua (Bolivia)
6. Dutch (Suriname)
7. Aymara (Paraguay)

118. FLORAL PRO(CON)FUSION

1. Water Lily
2. Christmas Orchid
3. Orchid
4. Kantuta
5. Rose
6. Ceibo
7. Chilean Bellflower
8. Kantuta
9. Ceibo
10. Cattleya Orchid

119. MUSICAL EXCESSES

1. Clop
2. Paw
3. Hint
4. Still
5. Pill
6. Raw
7. Roar
8. Boat
9. Jay
10. Wrap

120. REVOLUTIONARY WORDS

Jargon, Craftily, Warmed, Behaves

"If you tremble with indignation at every injustice, then you are a comrade of mine."

OTHER BOOKS IN THE SERIES

The Great India Challenge
PUZZLES, QUIZZES AND GAMES
Vinita Zutshi

With the 50 brainteasers in this fascinating book of puzzles, take a trip across numerous places, delve into an age-old history, try countless cuisines, meet a billion people and relish the adventure that is India!

ISBN: 9788184776669
Pages: 86

The Great World Challenge
Asia
Vinita Zutshi

How well do you know Asia? Test your knowledge of the largest continent in the world with puzzles, quizzes, mazes, word games, cross-outs, word searches and crosswords. Delve into puzzles that span the history, geography, culture, sports and politics of this continent to become an Asia-whiz. The Great World Challenge series of books have interesting quizzes on various regions of the world. This is the second in the series after the Great India Challenge that was published earlier.

ISBN: 9789351032830
Pages: 128

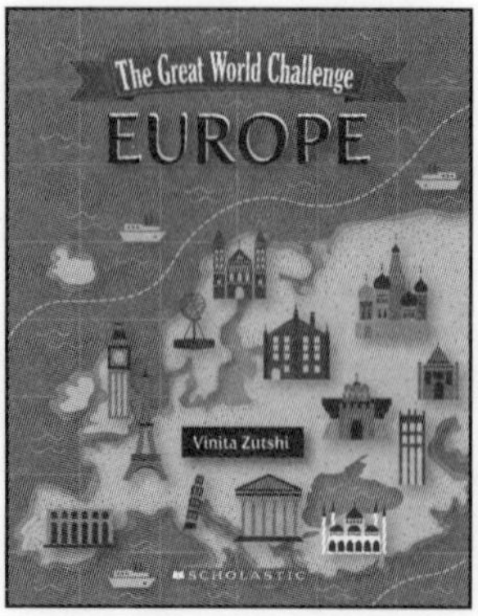

The Great World Challenge
Europe
Vinita Zutshi

Hop aboard the Eurail train, travel with intrepid explorers and revolutionary artists to discover mesmerising Europe. The 75 incredible brainteasers in this book will make you grab your seat (and possibly, a fellow traveller) as you delve into histories and cultures dating back to ancient times.

ISBN: 9789351039952
Pages: 132